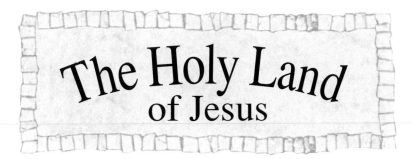

The Holy Land
of Jesus

Written by Don Achen

Illustrated with 375 pictures
by Israel's premier photographers

Doko Media

The Holy Land
of Jesus

Series Editor: Reuven Dorot
Written & Edited by: Don Achen
Design: Gal Kalderon

Photography: Albatross Aerial Photograhy Ltd. -
Dubi Tal & Moni Haramati, Eyal Bartov, Bouky Boaz, Lev Borodulin, Joel Fishman,
Itamar Grinberg, David Harris, Avi Hirschfield, Hanan Isachar, Garo Nalbandian,
Richard Nowitz, Ze'ev Radovan, Nitsan Shorer, Eitan Simanor, Israel Talby.
Illustrations + Map: Evgeny Barashkov
Satellite Map: Richard Cleave/Rohr Productions Ltd.

Published by Doko Media Ltd.
© Reuven Dorot / Shlomy Dayan.
ISBN: 965-478-054-2

Special thanks to the Israel Antiquities Authorities and the Israel Museum.

DOKO is Israel's leading production & distribution company for Biblical and historic
media products, publishing videos, books, CD ROM's & CD's, music cassettes.

For a free catalogue of our entire product range, please contact:

DOKO Entertainment Ltd.,
8, Ha'Amal St., POB 611 Or Yehuda. Israel 60371
Tel: 972 3 6344776 Fax: 972 3 6344690
e-mail: dokoe@attglobal.net
www.dokomedia.com

Contents

N

Mediterranean Sea

LEBANON

Sidon

Tyre
(Zor)

Caesarea Philippi
(Banias)

Golan
Heights

SYRIA

Galilee

Chorazin

The Mount of
the Beatitudes

Capernaum
Tabgh

Bethsaida

Akko
(Acre)

Sea of
Galilee

Cana

Tiberias

Haifa

Zippori

Nazareth

Mt. Tabor

Beth
Shearim

Nain

Jezreel Valley

Megiddo

Scytopolis
(Beth Shean)

Mt. Gilad

Caesarea

Samaria

Sebaste

JORDAN

Jerash

Sychar
(Shekem)

Jordan River

Amman

Antipatris

Tel-aviv
Jaffa

Jericho

Qumran

Ashdod

Jerusalem

Ein-Karem

Bethlehem

Madaba

Hebron

Dead
Sea

Mt. Moav

Gaza

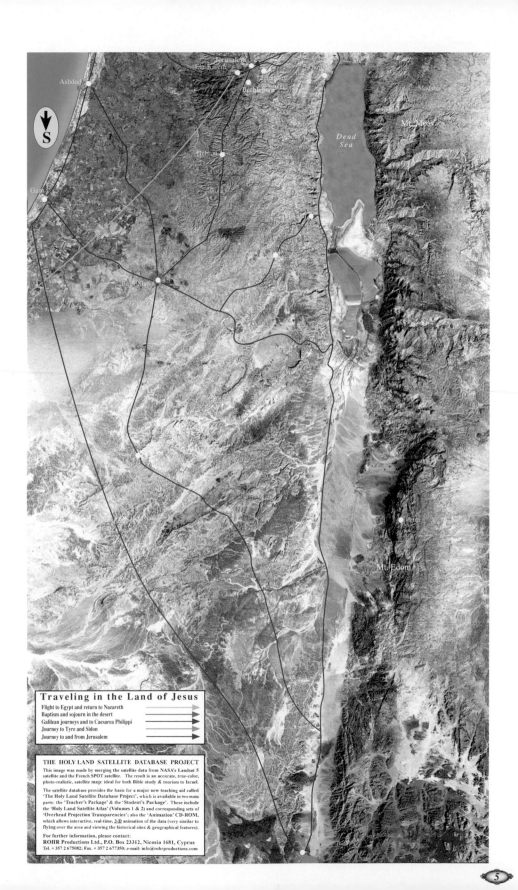

Jerusalem
Ein-Karem
Bethany
Bethlehem
Ashdod
Madaba
Mt. Moav
Dead
Sea
Hebron
Gaza
Beer-Sheva
Petra
Mt. Edom

Traveling in the Land of Jesus

Flight to Egypt and return to Nazareth
Baptism and sojourn in the desert
Galilean journeys and to Caesarea Philippi
Journey to Tyre and Sidon
Journey to and from Jerusalem

THE HOLY LAND SATELLITE DATABASE PROJECT

This image was made by merging the satellite data from NASA's Landsat 5 satellite and the French SPOT satellite. The result is an accurate, true-color, photo-realistic, satellite map: ideal for both Bible study & tourism to Israel.

The satellite database provides the basis for a major new teaching aid called 'The Holy Land Satellite Database Project', which is available in two main parts: the 'Teacher's Package' & the 'Student's Package'. These include the 'Holy Land Satellite Atlas' (Volumes 1 & 2) and corresponding sets of 'Overhead Projection Transparencies'; also the 'Animation' CD-ROM, which allows interactive, real-time, 3-D animation of the data (very similar to flying over the area and viewing the historical sites & geographical features).

For further information, please contact:
ROHR Productions Ltd., P.O. Box 23312, Nicosia 1681, Cyprus
Tel. + 357 2 675082; Fax. + 357 2 677350; e-mail: info@rohrproductions.com

FOREWORD

To know more about the land and history of the Bible is imperative to understanding the Bible itself. I encourage you to familiarize yourself with tools like this book to better your appreciation of the rich Jewish life of the first century, the very world Jesus knew so intimately. Familiarizing oneself with the lay of the land, it's customs and religious practices allows for deeper comprehension of the Text so dear to us.

To be a pilgrim in the places where our Lord lived and poured out His life is an experience of a lifetime. Treasuring those experiences by returning to those locations by means of the pictures, illustrations and descriptions contained here will repeatedly delight and thrill the reader.

Discovery and renewal are in store for you as you explore the Biblical sites with this aid, The Holy Land of Jesus. Let your heart be warmed and opened to fresh insights as the Scriptures come alive.

Understand better how formerly humble villages and surroundings were made world famous by the life and universal teachings of Jesus. How the One this book honors, has influenced this once remote area of the former Roman Empire, to now become the spiritual, economic and political crossroads for the last two millennia.

Come let us travel the dusty roads together. Be inspired by the views of Galilee and Jerusalem. Rejoice with the Psalmist at the majesty of His creation. Let us follow the Good Shepherd from Bethlehem, the carpenter of Nazareth, the Rabbi at Capernaum to the Savior at Golgotha and His ascension from the Mount of Olives.

Charles M. Kopp
Chairman,
United Christian Council in Israel.

*A*mong Christian circles, there is much talk today of the **History of Salvation**, meaning that God had worked through human history to bring redemption to mankind, particularly in the history of Israel and its most outstanding son Jesus Christ.

Still it is important to remember that there is not only a **History of Salvation** but also a **Geography of Salvation**. God has revealed himself by speaking to man in a rather limited region of the earth that is called **Holy Land**.

After living for over three decades in this land, I am convinced that a Christian, who desires to understand better the roots of his faith, can richly benefit by visiting the land where Jesus grew up, preached the Good News, suffered, died, and rose to a new life. I find that this book, written in a popular style but still well researched, can be of great help to prepare a projected visit to Israel/Palestine or convey a deeper appreciation of the sites after they had been visited. The author follows the sequence of the different events in the life of Christ, offering a short historical background for each holy place and elucidating them with a large spectrum of photos. I feel that reading this book attentively, it could widen your religious horizons and stretch out before you a panorama of faith and history, which will enrich your life.

Father Bargil Pixner OSB
Benedictine Monastery of Hagia
Maria Sion (Dormition Abbey)
Jerusalem

NAZARETH

The Flower of the Galilee

Nazareth is set among rolling Galilee hills covered with ancient groves of olive trees, overlooking the Jezreel valley. One of the oldest cities in the Holy Land, archaeological excavations of the area have found remains dating back some 3,000 years, to the time of the Bronze Age.

Nazareth was only a small village in the years of Jesus' childhood and youth, but its fame grew rapidly after his death. His early followers were called Nazarenes, and still today both the Hebrew and Arabic words for Christian - Notzri and Nazrani - are generally believed to be drawn from the town's name, in the same way as Jesus is often called Jesus of Nazareth. This name, given to Jesus in the New Testament is connected to the verse that talks of Joseph's return with his family to Nazareth *"And he came and dwelt in a city called Nazareth: that it might be fulfilled which was spoken by the prophets, He shall be called a Nazarene"*, Matthew 2:23.

However, the derivation of that word has long been the subject for debate. Since the

And in the sixth month the angel Gabriel was sent from God unto a city of Galilee, named Nazareth, To a virgin, espoused to a man whose name was Joseph, of the house of David; and the virgin's name was Mary. And the angel came in unto her, and said, Hail, thou art highly favoured, the Lord is with thee: blessed art thou among women.

Luke 1:26-28

4th century, scholars have pointed to the book of the prophet Isaiah as the probable source of the prophecy Matthew was referring to, *"And there shall come forth a rod out of the stem of Jesse, and a Branch shall grow out of his roots"*, Isaiah 11:1. Jesse was the father of King David, and branch is from the Hebrew word *"netzer"* meaning both shoot and descendent.

Designed to resemble a lighthouse, the Basilica of the Annunciation reflects one of the meanings of the town's name - Guardian- as it stands watch over the Jezreel Valley below. The church was erected over the ruins of five earlier churches built on the same spot.

It seems that Matthew is reinforcing the lineage of Jesus with which he opens his Gospel *"The book of the generation of Jesus Christ, the son of David, the son of Abraham"*, Matthew 1:1. Certainly, many scholars suggest that Jesus' royal line would be more important than the fact of coming from a tiny village in the Galilee that did not even warrant a mention in the Old Testament.

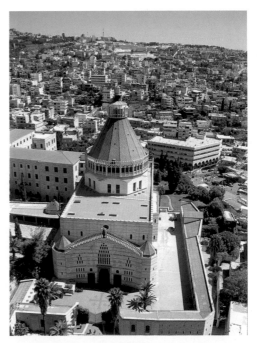

When Roberts first saw Nazareth, at the end of a journey up a long winding trail, he was so taken with the beauty of the small village sprawling around the Franciscan monastery, that he described it thus, "the beautiful hamlet of Nazareth nestled as it were in the bosom of the hills by which it is surrounded".

Dominated by the Basilica of the Annunciation, Nazareth was described by St. Jerome in the 4th century as "the Flower of the Galilee".

The Basilica of the Annunciation

The Basilica of the Annuciation is the largest of all the churches in the modern town of Nazareth. It celebrates the announcement brought to Mary by the angel Gabriel that she was to become the mother of the Messiah. Held by tradition to be part of the house of the family of Mary and the spot where she received the announcement, the first building erected over the sacred **Grotto of the Annunciation** was a church-synagogue used by the early Jewish-Christians. Later a Byzantine basilica was erected over the shrine, and this remained in use until the 12th Century.

Extensive excavations carried out in the 1950-60's revealed remains of the Byzantine church built in about 427, and a stone column on which the words "Ave Maria" were carved in antiquity, probably by a visiting pilgrim.

Destroyed and rebuilt many times, Nazareth was the Crusader capital of the Galilee in the 12-13th centuries. Tancred, the first Prince of the Galilee, rebuilt much of the town that he found in ruins.

Consecrated in 1969, the Basilica is famous for its stained glass windows and artwork donated by Christian communities from all over the world.

In 1263, the Mameluk leader Sultan Baybars, destroyed the great cathedral erected here by the Europeans. All that remains of that magnificent structure are several carved capitals depicting events of the life of Christ and the Crusader victory over the Moslems.

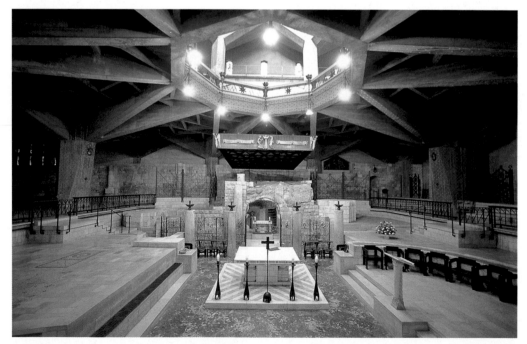

The crypt was constructed to preserve the remains of the two original churches built over the grotto. Inside, an inscription is still legible, "Verbum caro hic factum est" - Here the Word was made flesh.

When David Roberts visited Nazareth he painted the church the Franciscan Friars had built over the grotto in only seven months in 1730. This basilica was demolished in 1955 to make way for the present church.

Legend tells that when the Crusaders lost Nazareth to the Moslems in the 13th century, angels came down from heaven, picked up the church and transported it to the Italian village of Loretto near Ancona. Also known as *"Nazareth de Italia"* the local church there is called *"Santa Casa"* - the Holy House.

The beautifully carved capitals from Nazareth's great Crusader cathedral can be seen in the **Museum of the Basilica of the Annuciation**.
Please note that the museum closes every day between 12:00-14:00.

The carved columns made for the Crusader cathedral are among the country's finest examples of Romanesque art.

Archaeologists have unearthed the remains of Early Christians homes, part of the ancient village of Nazareth.

NAZARETH

Mary's Well

For thousands of years the well has been one of the focal points of village life. For men, this usually revolved around the importance of water to the irrigation of the fields. For the women whose job it was to care and tend for the flocks in times gone by, and still is in many agrarian cultures around the world, the importance of the village well was both practical and social.

The Old Testament tells us that the Patriarchs Isaac and Jacob found their respective wives, Rebecca and Rachel, as they were bringing their animals to the village well, Genesis 24 & 29. Later, the New Testament Gospel of John tells of a meeting between Jesus and a Samaritan woman that takes place at Jacob's Well in Nablus (see page 83).

Various traditions hold that the angel Gabriel first spoke to Mary by a well. They are based on the apocryphal gospels which

Built by the Crusaders in the 12th century, the Church of St. Gabriel was destroyed by Moslems a hundred years later. The present structure was erected as a Greek Orthodox church in 1781.

read, *"When the Virgin took the pitcher and went to draw water, behold a voice said to her: Hail, Mary full of grace.*

Tradition says that the angel Gabriel appeared to Mary as she was drawing water. Mary's Well is Nazareth's only spring, and is recognized by Orthodox Christians as the site where the Annunciation took place.

Mary saw no-one, but going into her house, while she was spinning purple wool, the angel appeared to her and said to her: Fear not, Mary ...".

For centuries, **Mary's Well** and the **Fountain of the Virgin** have been visited as the location of the event. The lines also gave the impetus for the building of **the Church of St. Gabriel** by the Crusaders in the 12th century. Although no hard

And the angel said unto her, Fear not, Mary: for thou hast found favour with God. And behold, thou shalt conceive in thy womb, and bring forth a son, and shalt call his name Jesus.
He shall be great, and shall be called the Son of the Highest; and the Lord God shall give him the throne of his father David: And he shall reign over the House of Jacob forever; and of his kingdom there shall be no end.

Luke 1:30-33

The fountain in the centre of Nazareth stands at a slight distance from the site David Roberts eagerly painted. The April 20 entry in his journal noted, "This fountain, with the groups of young women round it carrying their water jars, was more suited for a picture that anything I have seen in the Holy Land".

evidence exists, it is presumed by many that they were built on spots already hallowed by previous generations.

Other places of interest in Nazareth include **The Churches of the Copts** and **the Maronites**, the chapel known as **Mensa Christi** and **the White Mosque**, as well as **the Souk** - the market that is the centre of the town's commercial activities. Other sites in Nazareth connected to the life of Jesus can be found on pages 46/7 & 58/9.

Fed by water that rises in nearby Mary's Well, the Fountain of the Virgin was originally constructed in 1882 and thoroughly rebuilt in 1967.

13

EIN KAREM

The Church of the Visitation

Down the hill from Jerusalem's famed Hadassa Hospital sits the tranquil village of **Ein Karem**, Spring of the Vineyard, still set among the wooded hills on the outskirts of the city.

Although not mentioned by name, according to age-old tradition it was here that Mary came after the angel Gabriel informed her that her cousin, Elisabeth, was six months pregnant despite her advanced years. It was this visit that gave the main church of the village its name - **the Church of the Visitation**.

My soul doth magnify the Lord, and my spirit hath rejoiced in God my Saviour. For he hath regarded the low estate of his handmaiden: for, behold, from henceforth all generations shall call me blessed.

Luke 1:46-48

Luke's is the only gospel to describe the meeting between the two women in which Mary spoke the immortal words that we now know as the Magnificat. Decorated plaques engraved with the words in many languages adorn the walls of the courtyard of the church. They mark the meeting that took place in the home of Elisabeth and her husband Zachariah. His statue stands in the pleasant garden surrounding the church.

Zachariah was a priest in Jerusalem's Temple, and it was while he was on duty there that the angel Gabriel appeared to tell him of Elisabeth's imminent pregnancy. Zachariah was so unbelieving that he was struck dumb until

The Crusader grotto and courtyard and the original Franciscan building (1674) have all been skillfully integrated into the modern church.

The fresco celebrates the meeting between Mary and her aged cousin, Elisabeth, just outside Jerusalem.

the birth of their son, John, who grew up to become John the Baptist.

Inside the grotto in the church is a stone behind which it is said, the infant John hid when Herod sent out his troops to slaughter all the newborn infants of Bethlehem. Above the grotto's niche, a mural on the wall depicts the events of that awful day.

Close to the church in the center of the village is **the Spring of Our Lady Mary**, where the Virgin is said to have rested before the final climb to her cousin's house. Thirsty visitors still refresh themselves here with the well's cool waters.

Now an attractive suburb on the rural outskirts of Jerusalem, Ein Karem is a wonderful place to spend a peaceful day away from the bustle of the busy city, leisurely walking the streets with their artists' studios and galleries nestling beside ancient churches. Or one can make Ein Karem the base for a visit to Jerusalem, enjoying the hospitality of its hostels, such as the one at **the Convent of the Sisters of Sion**.

Above the grotto is an exquisitely decorated Franciscan church, designed by Antonio Barluzzi.

And Mary arose in those days, and went into the hill country with haste, into a city of Judah; And entered into the house of Zacharias, and saluted Elisabeth. And it came to pass, that when Elisabeth heard the salutation of Mary, the babe leaped in her womb; and Elisabeth was filled with the Holy Ghost: And she spake out in a loud voice, and said, Blessed art thou among women, and blessed is the fruit of thy womb.

Luke 1:39-42

EIN KAREM

The Church of St. John the Baptist

Each day, Ein Karem is filled with the chimes of church bells ringing out from every corner of this scenic village. One of its most impressive churches is **the Church of St. John the Baptist**, erected over the grotto where he is said to have been born.

Luke's gospel tells how the angel Gabriel described John to his father, Zachariah, saying, *"thy wife Elisabeth shall bear thee a son, and thou shall call his name John. And thou shall have joy and gladness; and many shall rejoice at his birth. For he shall*

be great in the sight of the Lord, and shall drink neither wine nor strong drink; and he shall be filled with the Holy Ghost".

Archaeological work nearby discovered a mosaic fragment dating back to the 5-6th century. Decorated with peacocks, partridges and flowers, it bears the Greek inscription *"Hail Martyrs of God".*

The connection of the village with John the Baptist was so strong that while the Latin Kingdom of Jerusalem flourished in the Holy Land, Ein Karem was known as St. John in the Mountains.

Set in pastoral surroundings, the Church of St. John the Baptist marks the traditional home of Elisabeth, where Mary stayed for three months.

This beautiful church is decorated with paintings depicting John the Baptist's short, but eventful life.

In Ancient Judea

Traditional methods of Agriculture.

Despite the tremendous advances in agricultural technology, traditional ways still thrive in many parts of the Holy Land. This creates a picture of village life much the same today as it was in the time of Jesus.

The sickle is the traditional tool for harvesting.

Wheat, barley and bread are mentioned in almost every book of the Bible - bread often being synonymous with teaching. Wheat is harvested with a sickle, the grain loosened from the ears on the threshing floor and then separated from the chaff using a winnowing fork to throw it in the air where the wind blows the lighter chaff aside.

Another crop dating back to antiquity is the olive. Always important, the multi-purpose olive was not only eaten, but its oil was used for cooking, for burning in lamps for lighting homes, for healing and to anoint the heads of the kings of Israel.

Olives were often crushed beneath heavy rolling stones to extract their precious oil.

Threshing is done with the help of donkey power.

A collection of ancient olive presses.

Other foods associated with the Holy Land include grapes and citruses, but perhaps the fruit most connected with this land is the apple. The Bible never actually says which was the forbidden fruit of the Garden of Eden, but for generations the apple has been depicted as the one that the serpent used to tempt Eve.

This beam press used stone weights to pull down on the beam and squeeze the oil from the olives.

Separating the wheat from the chaff.

David's Royal City

A few miles south of Jerusalem, near the edge of the Judean Desert, **Bethlehem** is built on a rocky prominence about 2500 feet (777m) above sea level. The town is surrounded by terraced hills covered with vineyards, olives, almonds and fig trees. Its name means *"House of Bread"* in Hebrew, and below the town are fields where the Old Testament book of Ruth recounts the unfolding story of her love with Boaz. Their son Obed became the grandfather of King David who was born and first anointed in Bethlehem three thousand years ago, 1 Samuel 16:13.

In the center of the town stands **the Church of the Nativity**, built over the traditional site of the manger where Jesus Christ was born. Matthew's gospel says that the birth took place here in

The view from the bell-tower above the Church of the Nativity.

order to fulfill the Old Testament prophecy, *"But thou Bethlehem Ephrata, though thou be little among the thousands of Judah, yet out of thee shall he come forth unto me that is to be ruler in Israel; whose goings forth have been from of old, from everlasting"*, Micah 5:2.

Erected over the grotto Bethlehem's Basilica has had a stormy history. In the year 135, following an abortive Jewish rebellion against Roman rule, the Emperor Hadrian attempted to wipe out all traces of the country's Messianic movement. He consecrated a shrine to the pagan god, Adonis, over the grotto. Ironically, this very act enabled locals to accurately guide visiting pilgrims directly to the spot almost two hundred years later.

Inspired by Queen Helena's pilgrimage to the Holy Land, the Emperor Constantine ordered the building of the Church of the Nativity in 326, over the cave of the manger.

Over the rooftops of the Church of the Nativity, the visitor gazes across to the stark mountains of Moab on the eastern side of the River Jordan.

Today's single low entrance to the church is called the "Door of Humility", as visitors have to stoop in order to enter.

And it came to pass in those days, that there went out a decree from Caesar Augustus, that all the world should be taxed. ... And all went to be taxed, everyone into his own city. And Joseph also went up from the Galilee, out of the city Nazareth, into Judea, unto the city of David, which is called Bethlehem; because he was of the house and lineage of David. To be taxed with Mary his espoused wife, being great with child.

Luke 2:1-5

Manger Square during the annual Christmas celebration.

When the Persians rampaged through the land in 614, destroying every sacred building that fell into their hands, the church was spared thanks to a mosaic depicting the Three Magi dressed in Persian garb.

In 1099, the Crusaders were welcomed as liberators when they took the city on their way to conquering Jerusalem. They returned to Bethlehem on Christmas Day the next year, 1100, to celebrate the coronation of Baldwin as the first King of Jerusalem.

The church used to have three entrances. Two have been completely blocked. The third and largest doorway - the outline of which is still clearly visible - was partially closed to prevent attacking horsemen riding straight into the church. This entrance is now known as the Door of Humility.

BETHLEHEM

The Church of Nativity

Entering **the Church of the Nativity** from busy Manger Square is like entering a different world. One is immediately struck by the atmosphere of timeless quality that permeates every corner of the vaulted basilica. Simple in every aspect of its construction, it is as beautiful as it is sacred.

At certain hours of the day the majestic pink limestone columns - each towering 6 meters - come to life when the sun, slanting through eleven high arched windows, seems to set them on fire. Above these columns are the remains of 12th century mosaics that once decorated the church. On a gold background they portray the forebears of Jesus and the first seven ecumenical councils.

Damaged through the years, most are only fragments of their originals, but the one portraying the Council of Constantinople of 680 has survived intact. It is a magnificent example of the art of its day.

Lined with red limestone pillars, the present Basilica is similar to the original 4th and 6th century churches built on this site.

A Silver Star marks the birthplace of Jesus. Inscribed on it are the words "Hic de Virgine Maria Jesus Christus natus est - Here Jesus Christ was born to the Virgin Mary".

Detail from the original 4th century mosaic floor discovered in 1934.

In modern times the idea of the manger has become associated with a place where animals are kept. In ancient times, however, the reality was more of a cave where fodder for the animals was stored - often along with other household goods. In fact, it has long been the practice in the region to build houses over caves - they being much warmer in the bitter winter and much cooler in the blistering heat of summer. The cave now under the basilica would have been a perfect choice.

On the lower part of many of the pillars are 14th and 15th century heraldic devices. Not frescoes, these are in fact works done employing the rare encaustic technique, which uses burned-in wax colors.

A small part of the flagstone floor in the nave of the basilica gives way to a wooden opening. This allows visitors to admire a section of the beautiful mosaic floor of Constantine's original 4th century church.

From either side of the basilica's great choir, flights of well-worn stairs lead down to **the Chapel of the Nativity**, located directly beneath the High Altar of the church.

In a small recess in the cave's wall, is the Altar of the Nativity. A Silver Star set in white marble marks the birthplace of Jesus, where millions come every year in reverence to the event that took place 2,000 years ago. Silver oil-lamps hang above it, burning night and day.

To the side of the grotto are two other altars; **the Chapel of the Crib**, where the newly born Jesus was laid, **and the Altar of the Magi**, in memory of the Three Wise Men who visited the babe in the Manger.

The Chapel of the Nativity contains the Altar of the Crib and the Altar of the Magi, all cut into the cave's rough stone.

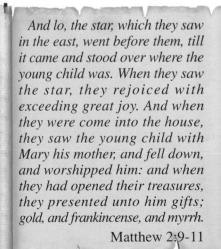

For generations pilgrims have looked to the pastures east of Bethlehem to find the location of **the Shepherds' Field**, where the first people on earth received the good news of the birth of Christ. Since no one location is universally accepted, various sites carry the title.

Many churches have been built in the area - one mosaic floor from Byzantine times can be seen in the Shepherds' Field church in the village of **Beit Shahour**.

In the grounds of the **Franciscan chapel**, excavations have revealed the ruins of an agrarian monastic center, with cisterns, silos and presses. Inhabited as far back as Herodian times, it had its heyday around the 6th century. The first church built here dates from the 4th or 5th century, and inscriptions upon the remains of two altars prove the enduring nature of the site's sacred character.

Shepherds still tend their sheep and goats in the fields surrounding Bethlehem. Note the hill of Herodion looming in the background.

One of the sites claiming the name Shepherds' Field, where many pilgrims gather to celebrate Christmas Eve.

And there were in the same country shepherds abiding in the field, keeping watch over their flock by night. And lo, the angel of the Lord came upon them, and the glory of the Lord shone round about them: and they were sore afraid.

And the angel said unto them, Fear not: for, behold I bring you good tidings of great joy, … For unto you is born this day in the city of David a Saviour, which is Jesus Christ the Lord. … And suddenly there was with the angel a multitude of the heavenly host praising God, and saying, Glory to God in the highest, and on earth peace, good will toward men.

Luke 2:8-14

Just outside Bethlehem, the village of Beit Sahour is one of the sites where tradition says the angel appeared to the shepherds. It is set among fields now used more for agriculture than for grazing.

The Church of St. Catherine

Thousands come every year to celebrate Christmas in Bethlehem, the birthplace of the Saviour. Many crowd into Manger Square, sing carols in Shepherds' Field or worship in **the Church of St. Catherine.**

Built in 1881, St. Catherine's is dedicated to the Egyptian martyr who died upon a wheel. Its grounds incorporate a Crusader cloister surrounding a peaceful courtyard with a statue of the 4th century church father, St. Jerome.

Beneath the courtyard is a series of underground caves connecting St. Catherine's to the Grotto of the Nativity. One cave was home to St. Jerome while he translated the Bible into Latin. Another houses a small chapel dedicated to the Innocent Children. This recalls the story told of Herod the Great in Matthew 2:16, *"Then Herod, when he saw that he was mocked by of the wise men, was exceeding wroth, and sent forth, and slew all the children that were in Bethlehem, and in all the coasts thereof, from two years old and under"*.

Seen around the world every Christmas Eve, the traditional Midnight Mass is broadcast from the Church of St. Catherine.

Dating from the time of the Crusader king, Baldwin II, this bishop's crosier was found at the Church of the Nativity in 1863.

Fortress palace of Herod the Great

Herod the Great was proclaimed King of Judea by the Roman Senate in 39 BC. However, he came to power only two years later at the end of a bloody war in which his Roman forces massacred women, children and the aged, and nearly destroyed Jerusalem and its Temple. This stamp of cruelty, the hallmark of Herod's reign, gives authenticity to Matthew's account of the Slaughter of the Innocent Children of Bethlehem, even though it is not mentioned in any other historical source.

Paranoid, afraid of attack from both without and from within, Herod built a series of fortified palaces. In 20 BC he began work on **Herodion**, a twelve and

Legend tells that when Herod the Great died, his son Archelaus had the body carried on a golden bier to Herodion for burial - but no traces of Herod's grave have ever been found.

Rising above the surrounding countryside, from the summit of the man-made hill of Herodion one can see the Dead Sea to the east and Jerusalem to the north.

a half acre fortress that overlooks the Judean Desert on one side and Bethlehem on the other.

When Herod died after a 35 year reign, an angel again appeared to Joseph telling him it was safe to return to Israel, Matthew 2:19-21. The Herod mentioned later in the Scriptures is his second son Herod Anitpas, who became ruler of the Galilee, including Nazareth.

BETHLEHEM

The Milk Grotto

Filled with artwork depicting the Madonna and Child, the small but ornate chapel of the Milk Grotto is dedicated to the nursing of the baby Jesus.

Behold, the angel of the Lord appeareth to Joseph in a dream, saying, Arise, and take the young child and his mother, and flee into Egypt, and be there until I bring thee word: for Herod will seek the young child to destroy him.

Matthew 2:13

In ancient times dreams were often seen as the voice of divine revelation. Thus it comes as no surprise that when Joseph was told by an angel to flee Bethlehem he followed the instructions given to him. According to the gospel of Matthew, at the same time Herod's troops were indeed being sent to slaughter all the city's male infants aged two years and under.

Tradition says that as the family left Bethlehem, they rested in a small cave not far from the Church of the Nativity. While Mary was suckling the baby Jesus, several drops of milk spilled to the floor, turning the whole cave milk-white and giving the site its name, **the Milk Grotto**.

Detail of one of the many shrines inside the Milk Grotto.

From as early as the fifth century a church dedicated to the Virgin Mother has stood at the site. The first chapel was probably built here by St. Paula, an aristocratic Roman widow who came to live in the Holy Land and helped establish some of its earliest monasteries.

For centuries the soft white stones from the Grotto were exported to the churches of Europe under the name of the Virgin's Milk. In our own days, nursing mothers of all denominations and of many religions come to the Milk Grotto to pray in the white stone cave. Believing in the cave's miraculous properties, they often take a piece of the soft rock to grind and add to their drinks.

A short walk from the Milk Grotto, one comes upon the 19th century Franciscan church called **the House of St. Joseph**. In the present-day chapel one can see evidence of the much earlier church - the lower layer of the apse built out of the virgin rock, and the base of the ancient altar.

It can be understood from the gospels that Holy Family did remain in Bethlehem for some time. After eight days the child Jesus was circumcised, as is the still the Jewish custom today, and after forty days Mary presented the child in the Temple in Jerusalem, Luke 2:21-22.

It is reasonable to assume that during such a long stay Joseph would have found a house in which to live. It is also relevant to point to Matthew's gospel that speaks of the three wise men having *"come into the house"*, to greet the newborn infant Jesus, Matthew 2:11. This line would seem to strengthen the idea of Joseph having a house in Bethlehem.

A serene statue at the entrance to the Milk Grotto captures the scene of the Holy Family setting out on their flight to Egypt.

THE FLIGHT TO EGYPT

The Gospel of Matthew is the only one to mention the flight to Egypt made by Joseph and Mary with the infant Jesus, or to recall the Old Testament verse *"Out of Egypt have I called my Son"* . He was referring to the prophecy made in the Book of Hosea 11:1.

Their journey across **the Sinai Desert** into Egypt, and their time in exile, followed the path of a tradition that goes back to the very roots of the Bible. The Old Testament book of Genesis tells of the journey made by the Patriarch Abraham to Egypt. He arrived in Canaan, still called Abram, and was promised the land by God: "*Abram journeyed, going on still toward the South. And there was a famine in the land: and Abram went down into Egypt to sojourn there; for the famine was grievous in the Land"*. Genesis 12:9-10.

Abraham's great-grandson Joseph, famous for his coat of many colours, was sold by his brothers and taken as a slave into Egypt. By interpreting Pharaoh's dreams, Joseph rose to become the most powerful man in the land after the king himself.

Now there arose a new king over Egypt, which knew not Joseph. And he said unto his people, Behold, the children of Israel are more and mightier than we. ...Therefore they did set over them taskmasters to afflict them with their burdens. And they built for Pharaoh treasure cities, Pithom and Raamses. ...And the Egyptians made the children of Israel to serve with rigour. And they made their lives bitter with hard bondage, in mortar and in brick.

Exodus 1:8-14

When famine again struck Canaan, Joseph's brothers also went down to Egypt. And so the Children of Israel came to dwell in Egypt, where they multiplied until *"there arose a new king over Egypt, which knew not Joseph"* . It is generally believed that this would have been the mighty pharaoh, Ramses II. Ramses reigned in 3,000 BC for 66 years, he sired 90 children and carved his name onto more colossal buildings than any pharaoh before or after him.

Fearful of their numbers, this Pharaoh ordered the Children of Israel to be enslaved and put them to work constructing Egypt's great cities. Then he ordered the sons of the Hebrews to be killed. One babe, however, was saved - set afloat in the Nile. He was rescued by a daughter of the Pharaoh who brought of the child up as her own. This was Moses, prince of Egypt.

Although the camel is the most common form of transport across the desert, the Holy Family is usually depicted riding on a donkey.

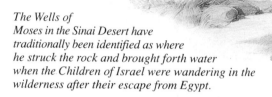

The Wells of Moses in the Sinai Desert have traditionally been identified as where he struck the rock and brought forth water when the Children of Israel were wandering in the wilderness after their escape from Egypt.

The savage beauty of the Sinai Desert is a mixture of bare craggy mountains, dry rocky valleys and endlessly shifting sand dunes.

Moses grew up to set his people free, leading them on the Exodus out of bondage and back across the **Sinai Desert** to the Promised Land.

The Sinai Desert is a 24,000 square mile land-bridge linking Africa with Asia. This wedge-shaped peninsula thrusts itself into the Red Sea creating the Gulfs of Suez to the southwest and Aqaba to the southeast. To the north it is bound by the Mediterranean Sea.

Its sparkling blue waters and long stretches of the bright yellow sand give the Sinai some of the most magnificent beaches in the region. Many of these, especially along the Gulf shore around **Ras Muhammed, Ras Burkha** and **Sharm el-Sheikh**, boast some of the most spectacular coral reefs in the world.

MOUNT SINAI

And Santa Catherina

The Exodus out of Egypt led the Children of Israel across the Sinai Desert, where Moses had first encountered God's presence in the Burning Bush. Many traditions surround the mountains of Sinai, each associated with a different episode of the Bible.

Jebel Musa, at 7,500 feet (2270m), is generally identified as **Mount Sinai** itself, the peak Moses climbed to receive the Ten Commandments from God.

A path of 3,000 steps leads up to the summit of the mountain. In ages past,

There were thunders and lightnings, and a thick cloud upon the mount, and the voice of the trumpet exceedingly loud; so that all the people that was in the camp trembled. And Moses brought forth the people out of the camp to meet with God; and they stood at the nether part of the mount. And Mount Sinai was altogether on a smoke, because the Lord descended upon it in fire: and the smoke thereof ascended as the smoke of a furnace, and the whole mount quaked greatly. And when the voice of the trumpet sounded long, and waxed louder and louder, Moses spake, and God answered him by a voice. And the Lord came down upon mount Sinai, on the top of the mount: and the Lord called Moses up to the top of the mount; and Moses went up.

Exodus 19:16-20

climbing these steps was the penitence given to pilgrims to achieve forgiveness - and serious sinners were sometimes even instructed to climb the mountain on their knees! On one's feet it is a climb that takes about three hours, but it is one that is richly rewarded. On a clear day there is a spectacular view across the Gulf of Aqaba to the coast of Saudi Arabia.

On his experience of Mount Sinai, David Roberts' journal reads, *"Near the top are small chapels, one covers the cave where Elijah was fed by the ravens and the other is dedicated to Elias and on the summit are two others; one where Moses received the tables of the law and the other belongs*

Though the exact location of the Biblical Mount Sinai remains unknown, tradition places it at Jebel Musa – the Mountain of Moses - in the central highlands of the Sinai Peninsula.

to the Mohamedans; immediately under it is pointed out the footmark of the camel that carried him from Mount Ararat to Mecca. The view from the top is the most sublime that can be imagined".

Sitting more than 5,000 feet (1515m) above sea level, **the Monastery of Santa Catherina** - St. Catherine - is the most striking feature in the area of Mount Horeb. Built in the 6th century by the Fathers of Sinai, the monastery is dedicated to the martyr of Alexandria who died in 395.

The courtyard of St. Catherine's caught David Roberts' eye, but it was "the attention and kindness with which we have been treated during our stay" that caught his heart.

This Greek Orthodox monastery, the smallest diocese in the world, holds one of the greatest collections of religious texts and paintings. Among its 4,500 priceless manuscripts the monastery claims possession of the "*Codex Sinaiticus*", believed to be the oldest translation of the Bible in the world, and over 2,000 ancient icons.

The highest peak in all Sinai is the **Mountain of St. Catherine**. At 8,650 feet (2620m) it is a good five-hour climb. Legend says that when St. Catherine was killed, her body was borne away by angels who brought it back to earth on the top of this mountain - five centuries later! A small chapel marks the spot at the mountain's summit.

The monastery of Santa Catherina sits at the base of the imposing cliffs of Mount Horeb, site of Moses' encounter with the Burning Bush.

Sinai's rugged mountains are surrounded by sandy beaches and the clear blue waters of the Red Sea.

MOUNT CARMEL

Elijah's Cave & the Mukhraka

Mount Carmel is a limestone range that stretches for almost 16 miles southwards from the modern city of Haifa. It is here that we find **Elijah's Cave**, also known to the Christian world as **the Cave of Madonna**. Legend has it that the Holy family found shelter here on their return to the Holy Land from Egypt.

But the history of the Carmel stretches much farther back into the very mists of time. Scattered along the heights overlooking the Mediterranean Sea, numerous caves have been found containing human remains dating back 100,000 years to the middle period of the Old Stone Age.

In the caves of **the Nachal Hamearot Nature Reserve** some of the earliest examples of human habitation in the world are on public display.

In Biblical times the heights of the Carmel mountains were considered the seat of Baal, one of the main gods worshipped by the Canaanite peoples of the region. When the Jewish turned to wickedness and started following Baal, the prophet Elijah punished them by causing a drought to come upon the land. Then the famous mountaintop confrontation took place on the Carmel between the prophet Elijah and 450 priests of Baal. Calling upon the people to return from evil and follow the one true God, Elijah challenged the priests to have Baal himself ignite their altar. They failed, and Elijah built an altar of his own, had twelve barrels of water poured over it, and then called on God to ignite it.

The ancient Canaanites saw the wild summit of the Carmel mountain range as the dwelling place of their god, Baal.

Man's earliest ancestors once inhabited many of the caves in the Nachal Hamearot Nature Reserve.

Inside and outside the cave of Elijah

God did so, as it is recorded, *"Then the fire of the Lord fell, and consumed the burnt sacrifice, and the wood, and the stones, and the dust, and licked the up water that was in the trench"*. 1 Kings 18:38.

This event took place at the southern end of the range at a spot called **the Mukhraka**, a name taken from the Arabic word for burn. A statue of Elijah stands at the site, upon a base decorated with details of the event. A monastery erected by the Carmelite order stands nearby.

The biographer of Pythagoras, the famed Greek mathematician of the 6th century BC and founder of the esoteric school of Samos called the *"Semicircle"*, states that the philosopher often came to the Holy Land *"to meditate in the sacred place of Carmel"*.

HEBRON

The Tomb of the Patriarchs

One of the most ancient settlements of the Holy Land, the city of **Hebron** is referred to in the Old Testament both by that name and as Kyriat Arba - City of the Four, after the confederation of four local towns.

Situated in a fertile region of the Judean Hills, it was to Hebron that Moses sent twelve spies to scout out the area when the Children of Israel approached Canaan on their way back from Egypt to the Promised Land.

Most returned with reports of a land flowing with milk and honey, one in which a bunch of grapes grew so large that it had to be carried on a pole held by two strong men. But some scouts came back fearful of the local population, and reported that giants inhabited the land, Numbers 13.

Led by Joshua, whose bravery quelled their fears, the people did manage to conquer Canaan, and slowly forged the twelve tribes into a nation. Centuries later, David - the shepherd boy who killed the Philistine giant, Goliath, with his sling - was brought to Hebron to be anointed king over the combined kingdoms of Judah & Israel, the southern and northern parts of the country. David made Hebron his capital for seven years.

The Tomb of the Patriarchs

Venerated by Jews, Christians and Moslems alike, the Tomb of the Patriarchs has its

This painting by David Roberts shows how Hebron has always been dominated by the Tomb of the Patriarchs.

At the heart of the Tomb are two large mausoleums dating from the 9th century. Tradition says the one on the right is Abraham's, while that on the left is Sarah's.

In the Second Temple period, Herod the Great added to the Tomb hoping to win the favour of his Jewish subjects. He built the powerful outer wall, giving it more than just the appearance of a fortress - its walls are actually eight and a half feet thick!

Following the conquest of the land by the Mameluks in the 12th century, the town became known by its Arabic name of Al- Khalil, meaning The Friend. The name stems from the title given to Abraham - the father of the Arab nation through his first son Ishmael - who is called Al-Khalil el-Rahman, the Friend of the Lord. Likewise, the tomb itself is known to the Arab world as Haram el-Khalil, the Sanctuary of the Friend.

roots in antiquity. According to the Book of Genesis, it was in Hebron that the Patriarch Abraham – till then a wandering nomad - purchased his first plot of land in Canaan. It was a field containing the cave of the Machpelah, that he bought as a tomb in which to bury his deceased wife, Sarah, Genesis 23:4-20.

Built over the Cave of the Machpelah, today the Tomb of the Patriarchs serves as a synagogue and mosque - but the Cave is visible only through a small opening in the wall.

Later, when Jacob died in Egypt, Joseph led his brothers back to Canaan to bury their father in the Machpelah cave next to his grandparents, Abraham and Sarah, his parents, Isaac and Rebecca, and his first wife, Leah. These are the Patriarchs buried in the tomb.

RACHEL'S TOMB

Rachel was the second and favourite wife of Jacob. He married her older sister Leah, first, because of a trick played on him by her father, as told in Genesis 29.

Rachel is the only one of the Patriarchs and Matriarchs not to be buried in Hebron, and we are told that she died giving birth to her second son, Benjamin, while on the road to Bethlehem - and that Jacob placed a marker on the spot. Revered by followers of the regions three monotheistic religions, **Rachel's Tomb** has become a popular place of pilgrimage. Through the centuries it has come to hold a special place in the

Rachel's Tomb is on the road between Bethlehem and modern-day Efrat, south of Jerusalem.

A magnet to pilgrims, the covered passage leading into the tomb was opened by Moses Montefiore in 1841.

hearts of women, and Jewish women especially come here to pray for fertility and for the healthy birth of their children.

The Gospel of Matthew 2:16-18 states that Herod's slaughter of the innocent children in Bethlehem was the fulfillment of an earlier prophecy, *"A voice was heard in Ramah, lamentation, and bitter weeping; Rachel weeping for her children refused to be comforted"*, Jeremiah 31:15.

The small white-domed tomb probably dates originally from the Crusader period, but most of the present building is fifteenth century construction, with later additions.

Israel is a tiny strip of fertile land along the coast of the Mediterranean Sea surrounded on three sides by huge, harsh deserts. Because of the area's intrinsic lack of water, from time immemorial man has been forced to come up with inventive ways of capturing and storing every drop of rain that falls in the Levant's brief winter.

Once in the capital, the water was stored in underground cisterns like **the Struthion Pools** that can still be seen beneath the Convent of the Sisters of Zion, by the Ecce Homo arch (pages 136/7). This was insurance against drought or siege - both of which constantly threatened the city.

The Struthion Pools pre-date Herod, probably having been originally built by Hyrcanus, the Hasmonean king who ruled in the 2nd century BC. The Emperor Hadrian added the Pools' vaulted ceiling in 135 AD.

Dating back 2,000 years, these man-made reservoirs were so important throughout the history that in the 17th century the Turks built a castle nearby just to protect them. Though the Pools are still in good condition, of Qala' at el Burak - the Castle of the Pools - only ruins remain.

Called **the Pools of Solomon** even though most modern scholars believe that they were more likely built during the reign of that grand architect, Herod the Great, these three ancient reservoirs are both beautiful, and vital.

Capturing the precious rainfall across a large catchment area of the hills of Judea, the flat-bottomed pools held the water until times of the all too frequent drought. It was then released to flow along stone pipes and extensive aqueducts that carried it all the way to Jerusalem, twelve and a half miles away.

Underground cisterns like this one stored water throughout the capital.

Of the Bedouin

Well before the time of Abraham, wandering tribes of nomads inhabited the desert lands that stretch across huge areas of the Near East. Today, the only people that preserve this age-old traditional way of life are the tribes of Moslem Arabs called the **Bedouin**.

The Bedouin are shepherds, constantly flowing back and forth with their flocks across the man-made borders of modern nation-states. They are driven from place to place by the never-ending need for new grazing land for their sheep and goats. In a few areas, such as Israel's Negev Desert, there is enough rainfall to allow for a brief winter wheat harvest without the need for further irrigation. This often gives Bedouin families the possibility to grow enough grain to supply their daily needs.

With their animals' wool they weave tents and rugs and - in times gone by - their clothing too, especially the women's embroidered dresses. Nowadays, more and more Bedouin tend to trade their traditional handicrafts in the local markets, and purchase mass-produced clothes for the whole family. Modern Bedouin can be seen in the **Beersheba Market** that takes place on Thursday mornings in the south of the town. Exhibitions of their cultural history, along with the history of the Negev, can be explored in the **Negev Museum** nearby.

Despite the pressures of the modern world that are causing more and more Bedouin to leave their nomadic ways and set down permanent roots, these people actively preserve their old and multi-faceted culture.

Playing music on simple, hand-made instruments, they accompany the evening's hospitality in their tents. Traditional story telling around the fire is punctuated by the rhythmic grinding of coffee that is served all night long. Many of these stories, passed down from generation to generation, contain teachings of honour, righteousness and the deeds of their ancestors, like the Patriarch Abraham - Ibrahim, as they call him. The stories are an intrinsic part of the way the Bedouin keep alive their rich and proud heritage.

AVDAT

A city on the Nabatean Spice Route

Although **Avdat** today appears to be in the middle of the bare, inhospitable wilderness of the Negev Desert, 2,000 years ago it was a thriving market town in the midst of an intensely cultivated agricultural area. The secret was a method of "water harvesting" developed, some believe, by the ancient Nabateans.

Water harvesting is an ingenious system of collecting every drop of winter rain that falls onto the impenetrable desert ground. Man-made channels cross kilometers of the bare hillsides, carrying water to reservoirs cut into the living rock. Alternatively the channels lead the water to a long series of small dams in the valleys so that it can slowly permeate into the earth giving sustenance to crops throughout a short growing season. By these methods huge tracts of land were cultivated and the Negev remained a thriving economic and highly populated region for several hundred years.

Established by the Nabateans as early as the 4th century BC, most of the structures now visible on Avdat's acropolis date from the 6th century Byzantine city that flourished here. Clearly visible below the summit are some of the many caves around which private houses were erected.

The Nabateans were a nomadic people who appeared on the map of history around the 6th century BC, in the deserts of northern Arabia in what is now the Kingdom of Jordan. They considered themselves the descendents of one of the twelve sons of Ishmael - the son of Abraham and Hagar, and the father of all the Arab nations, Genesis 16:15.

The first to harness the power of the camel for long-range commerce, the Nabateans quickly came to dominate the course of trade known as the Spice Route. This was the route that brought incense and spices from the East to the great civilizations that developed around the Mediterranean Sea - Egypt, then Greece and later Rome.

Known collectively as the Perfumes of Arabia, these precious commodities were in such high demand in the temples and palaces of antiquity that the camel caravans often comprised over a thousand animals - each one carrying up to half a ton of goods on its back!

To protect this valuable merchandise from marauding bandits, the Nabateans built a series of stations along the route from their capital of Petra through to the Mediterranean port-city of Gaza. Much like the stations of the Pony Express in the Wild West, these caravanserai were a days ride apart, and provided a bath and a bed for the night for the caravan masters, and water and fodder for their beasts. Avdat is one of the oldest of the stations, and grew to be one of the largest, along with the settlements of **Halutza, Mamshit, Nizana** and **Shifta.**

A modern camel caravan rests in the southern desert. Rich camel masters may have been the Three Wise Men who brought gold, frankincense and myrrh to the newborn Jesus in the Manger.

This doorway led into one of the two large Byzantine churches that dominated Avdat towards the end of its era of greatness. They were built on the sites of earlier Nabatean temples dedicated to the gods Dushara (Zeus) and El-Uzza (Aphrodite).

PETRA

In the Hashemite Kingdom of Jordan
The Nabatean capital

Hidden deep in the mountainous canyons of Jordan sixty miles north of the Gulf of Aqaba, **Petra**, the Rose-red city of the Nabatean is unique in the world. Their whole capital was hewn out of soft, pink sandstone rock: temples, amphitheater, tombs and homes.

Situated in the centre of the region the Bible calls Edom, Petra can only be reached down the long, narrow and winding ravine called the Siq. With perhaps the best natural defence in the world, Petra grew to command the trade routes crossing Arabia, and was able to hold out against the envious armies of the most successful empires of her day.

In 312 BC the Nabateans repulsed the heirs to Alexander the Great, and in 63 BC they even managed to maintain their independence against the most brilliant of all Roman generals, Pompey, as he advanced to take possession of the entire region.

The Nabateans were finally subdued only in 106 AD. With trade along the spice route at its height, Rome could no longer allow such a profitable source of wealth to remain in independent hands. The Emperor Trajan sent his forces to defeat the Nabatean army far from their impregnable stronghold in Petra, and annex their kingdom into Provincia Arabia.

Despite the defeat, Petra continued to thrive as a vassal to Rome, and many archaeologists believe it is their influence that is seen both in the city's architecture and in the run-off irrigation systems used throughout the region.

Petra appears suddenly at the end of the Siq gorge.

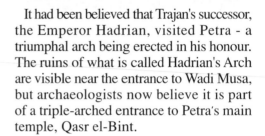

Two views of the Petra's ornate treasury, symbol of its position as the dominant emporium of antiquity.

It had been believed that Trajan's successor, the Emperor Hadrian, visited Petra - a triumphal arch being erected in his honour. The ruins of what is called Hadrian's Arch are visible near the entrance to Wadi Musa, but archaeologists now believe it is part of a triple-arched entrance to Petra's main temple, Qasr el-Bint.

By the Byzantine period, the Nabateans had lost their power, and Petra had lost its inhabitants. A small group of Christians converted many of Petra's temples into Christian places of worship. By the time of the Islamic expansion into the area, Petra was already a forgotten backwater of civilization. Rediscovered by the Crusaders, it fell again into obscurity until a young 19th century Swiss adventurer, Johann Burkhardt, brought knowledge of it back to the West.

Petra's magnificent amphitheater seated over 7,000 spectators on 33 rows of stone seats.

El Khasne Farun - its name, meaning Pharaoh's Treasury, stems from a legend that tells of treasure hidden inside .

midst of the doctors, both hearing them, and asking them questions. And all that heard him were astonished at his understanding and answers", Luke 2:42-46.

Upon the death of Herod the Great, the kingdom was divided between Herod Antipas, Archelaus and Philip, three of the numerous sons born to his nine wives.

Cast in the same mould as his father, Archelaus took over rule of the area that included Jerusalem. Finding the capital in turmoil, he sent in troops to establish control. This sparked a riot in which the crowds turned on the soldiers, stoning them to death. Enraged, Archelaus sent in the rest of his army, and 3,000 Jews died in the bloody massacre that followed.

By sharp contrast, there was peace in the northern areas where Antipas and Philip ruled. And it was to Nazareth in the Galilee that Matthew's gospel tells us Joseph came to make a new home for the family on their return from Egypt. Modern excavations have shown that Nazareth was just a modest hamlet, 2,000 years ago. With a population of only a few hundred souls, Joseph would probably have had a good social standing as a carpenter among his less educated neighbours.

This view seems confirmed by the Talmud, the compilation of the Jewish law, which indicates that where a community has no Rabbi (teacher) the carpenter, or the carpenters son, may be consulted on matters of religious law.

This shines an interesting light on the scriptural passage that tells of Jesus' early visit to Jerusalem's great Temple, *"And when he was twelve years old, they went up to Jerusalem as was the custom of the feast. And when they had fulfilled the days, as they returned, the child Jesus tarried behind in Jerusalem; and Joseph and his mother knew not of it. ...*
And it came to pass, that after three days they found him in the temple, sitting in the

Built on the traditional site of his workshop, St. Joseph's Church covers the remains of a 6th century structure.

This ancient mosaic was found when building the crypt of the present church. It may have been a ritual bath, perhaps used by Nazareth's early Judeo-Christian community.

Built in 1914, **the Church of St. Joseph** is found in the compound of the Basilica of the Annunciation. It was constructed over caves that may have been storerooms, cisterns or lower rooms incorporated into the houses of Nazareth's ancient village. St. Joseph's is the church most often visited as the site of Joseph's home and workshop. However, the title is contested by both St. Gabriel's and **the Convent of the Sisters of Nazareth** - which also contains a tomb popularly called the Tomb of St. Joseph, although Jewish tradition would have forbidden burial inside the town.

But when Herod was dead, behold, an angel of the Lord appeared in a dream to Joseph in Egypt, saying, Arise, and take the young child and his mother, and go into the land of Israel; for they are dead that sought the young child's life. And he arose, and took the young child and his mother, and came into the land of Israel.
But when he heard that Archelaus did reign in Judea in the room of his father Herod, he was afraid to go thither; notwithstanding, being warned of God in a dream, he turned aside into the parts of Galilee: and he came and dwelt in a city called Nazareth.
Matthew 2:19-23

Although not mentioned in the Old or the New Testaments, the city of **Sepphoris** was under reconstruction when Jesus lived in Nazareth, just five miles away. Several Christian traditions suggest this was the hometown of Mary, the mother of Christ, and point to various buildings as being associated with her parents, Anne and Joachim.

As the capital of the Western Galilee, warring armies looking for control of the area were always overrunning Sepphoris. In the winter of 39-8 BC Herod the Great seized it during a mid-winter snowstorm, on his way to storming Jerusalem. After his death, the city rebelled against Roman occupation and was destroyed. His son, Herod Antipas rebuilt the city, but the Romans occupied it again during the First and the Second Jewish Revolts, giving it the Roman name Diocaesarea.

Only when the Jewish leadership promised to refrain from attempts to throw off Roman rule did Jewish life return to some semblance of normality.

With Jerusalem's temple destroyed, the synagogue became the chief place of worship, and the Sanhedrin - the Jewish High Court - moved to Sepphoris. Here, under leadership of the renowned scholar, Juda Hanassi, the Oral Law was codified into the Mishna, laying the foundations for the normative Judaism that has survived through to own day.

Under Byzantine rule Sepphoris flourished, with many large villas being constructed. Many of these patricians' homes are still being uncovered, others have already revealed some of the country's most magnificent mosaics. One is titled *"the Birth of the Nile"* and another, containing a face of haunting beauty, has been dubbed *"the Mona Lisa of the Galilee"*.

Sepphoris, the Latin name for the Galilee city of Zippori, is still being excavated. Long dominated by a hilltop stronghold, the present one was raised by Daher el Omar in the 18th century, but built from materials taken from earlier fortifications.

Detail of one of the magnificent mosaics found at Sepphoris. Mosaics reached their zenith as an art form in the Byzantine period, appearing in churches and synagogues as well as private houses.

In Crusader times Sepphoris was a well-watered and fortified position. It was here that the young king, Guy de Lusignan, assembled his full force of Frankish knights to face the summer incursions of Saladin. A Kurd at the head of the greatest Moslem army ever gathered against the Crusaders, Saladin had laid siege to the Castle of Tiberias, with the Lady of Tiberias captive inside. Facing political factions that were just waiting for him to fail, Guy took the fatal decision to move against the superior Arab army. Harassed at every step as they moved towards Tiberias, the Crusaders camped for the night by wells at the double-hill dubbed **the Horns of Hattin**, only to find them completely dry.

By just after noon on Saturday, July 4, 1187, the young man who had barely ruled for twelve months had lost his entire fighting force of Crusader knights, the most important remnant of the True Cross, and the whole of his kingdom. After three months, Saladin had occupied the land and bloodlessly retaken Jerusalem. This was the end of the Latin Kingdom of Jerusalem that had lasted less than ninety years.

This mosaic portrait of a beautiful young woman has become known as the Mona Lisa of the Galilee.

The Baptismal sites: Yardenit & Qasr el Yehud

Fed in the north by melting snows from Mount Hermon and finishing its journey in the Dead Sea, **the River Jordan** takes over 200 miles to flow a distance that is only 65 miles as the crow flies. Despite its modest length the Jordan is one of the best known rivers in the world.

All four Gospels mark Jesus' baptism by his cousin, John the Baptist, who had been preaching repentance and preparing the way, saying, *"I indeed baptize you with water; but one mightier than I cometh, the latchet of whose shoes I am not worthy to unloose: he shall baptize you with the Holy Spirit and with fire"*, Luke 3:16.

Pilgrims come from all over the world to take part in a ceremony that is as old as Christianity itself.

The event took place in the Jordan River, and for generations baptism in its waters has been a central part of the pilgrim's journey to the Holy Land. But different Christian traditions developed through the ages pointing to two spots on the western bank of the river as being where Jesus' baptism occurred. The older tradition is maintained by the Orthodox Church at **Qasr el Yehud**, the Castle of the Jews, named in memory of the day Joshua led the Children of Israel across the Jordan River into the Promised Land.

Throughout the centuries huge crowds have gathered here to mark the Epiphany - the day that commemorates the baptism of Jesus.

The Yardenit is situated where the Jordan River leaves the Sea of Galilee.

Other pilgrims choose to be baptized at the more northerly site of **Yardenit**. Built especially for the purpose at the point where the Jordan exits the Sea of Galilee, Yardenit was established in our own generation.

A new site is now hoping to draw pilgrims as the true place of the original baptism. It is on the eastern, Jordanian side of the river, not far from the ruins of another Byzantine church.

Then cometh Jesus from Galilee to Jordan unto John, to be baptized of him. But John forbad him, saying, I have need to be baptized of thee, and comest thou to me? And Jesus answering said unto him, Suffer it to be so now: for thus it becometh us to fulfill all righteousness. Then he suffered him. And Jesus, when he was baptized, went straightway out of the water: and lo, the heavens were opened unto him, and he saw the Spirit of God descending like a dove, and lighting upon him: And lo a voice from heaven, saying, This is my beloved son, in whom I am well pleased.
Matthew 3:13-17

The Greek Orthodox monastery of St. Jerasimos, known in Arabic as Deir Hajla, was first settled in Byzantine times around 455 AD.

Crowds from many denominations line the banks of the Jordan on the occasion of the Epiphany.

The Monastery of the Temptation

The Quarantal - from *"quarantena"* meaning forty - takes its name from the forty days and nights Jesus spent in the wilderness after his baptism in the Jordan River.

The Monastery of the Temptation at Quarantal overlooks the town of Jericho in the Judean Desert. Built onto the sheer face of the mountain, it stands over the cave tradition recognizes as the place Jesus spent those days in fasting and meditation. The grotto is now a small chapel called **the Chapel of the First Temptation.** Its altar was erected over the stone where Jesus is said to have sat while he fasted.

The traditional way to the monastery is on foot up the narrow winding path, but recently a comfortable new cable car was installed allowing access to visitors of all ages who wish to see the beautiful monastery and the site of the temptation of Christ.

And Jesus being full of the Holy Ghost returned from Jordan, and was led by the Spirit into the wilderness, being forty days tempted of the devil. And in those days he did eat nothing: and when they were ended, he afterward hungered. And the devil said unto him, If thou be the Son of God, command this stone that it be made of bread. And Jesus answered him, saying, It is written, that man shall not live by bread alone, but by every word of God.

Luke 4:1-4

The present monastery is Greek Orthodox, built in the 19th century over the ruins of an earlier church. The monastic way of life has been followed here for millennia, but records of the tradition of climbing Mount Quarantal date back only as far as the Crusader period, to the 12th and 13th centuries.

The Quarantal's austere lines reflect the lives of simplicity, meditation and fasting followed by monks drawn here since the dawn of the Christian era.

At the walled summit over 550 feet high (170m), by the ruins of a Byzantine and Medieval church, is the **Chapel of the Third Temptation**. This marks the high place where the devil offered to give Jesus dominion over all the world, if Jesus would worship him. Jesus answered with the immortal words, *"Get thee behind me, Satan: for it is written, Thou shalt worship the Lord thy God, and him only shalt thou serve"*, Luke 4:8.

MAR SABA

With sky-blue domes and red-tiled roofs, **the Monastery of Mar Saba** is a striking example of the monastic communities that made their homes in the Judean wilderness.

The mountains are honeycombed with caves where early Christian hermits retreated into solitude. Slowly they came together, carving communities out of the rock, and the first monasteries were built in the early centuries of the first millennium.

Mar Saba was established by the 5th century saint, director of all the hermits living in the Judean desert. Attacked during the Persian invasion of 614, forty monks were martyred here. Twenty more were killed during Mar Saba's "Golden Age", two hundred years later. This led to the construction of protective towers. The Crusaders brought a

Founded in 482, the monastery of Mar Saba hangs over the gorge of Wadi en Nar, the Valley of Fire.

short-lived peace that was replaced by the constant harassment of marauding bandits. And if the hand of man had not done damage enough, an earthquake destroyed almost the entire complex in 1834. It was rebuilt in it present form with Russian help in the 1840's.

Inside, heaps of skulls of the martyred monks can be seen. Also worthy of a visit is the cell of the 7th century church scholar, St. John Damascene - a mighty defender of Orthodoxy and mysticism. His persuasive arguments in favour of using images in religious places promoted the tradition of Eastern icons, and led to the nurturing of some of the West's most gifted artists by the Renaissance Church.

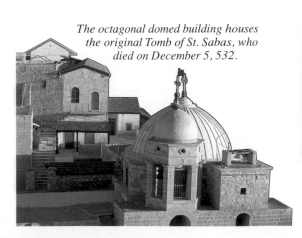

The octagonal domed building houses the original Tomb of St. Sabas, who died on December 5, 532.

The interior of St. Sabas' tomb is one of the most impressive examples of traditional Greek Orthodox art.

QUMRAN
And the Dead Sea Scrolls

After the discovery of scrolls in nearby caves, a score of buildings were unearthed inside a walled precinct watched over by a high tower. No living quarters were found however for this was a centre for people who lived in surrounding caves, huts and tents.

Qumran's first archaeologists saw it as the 1st century BC home of a peaceful, "monastic" sect of Jews called Essenes. Although still widely accepted, this view has been at the heart of a bitter controversy for over fifty years. Some opponents see the community as a military outpost or a fortified agricultural settlement. Others say the scrolls were spirited out of Jerusalem away from the advancing Roman army, and hidden in the desert for safety. All point out that no monastic tradition exists in Judaism - it developed in later Christianity. Perhaps future discoveries will reveal a clearer picture of the community's purpose and its inhabitants.

Part of the 8-meter long "Temple Scroll", found in 1967 under the floor tiles of a Bethlehem antiquities dealer.

Dubbed an "Essene monastery" fifty years ago, scholars are now divided over who lived here.

According to the words of Luke's Gospel, John the Baptist grew up in the desert. Some speculate that he might have been brought up in the isolated community at **Qumran**, twenty-five miles southeast of Jerusalem, by the Dead Sea.

And the child grew, and waxed strong in spirit, and was in the desert till the day of his shewing unto Israel.

Luke 1:80.

Copies of almost eight hundred manuscripts were found in the caves - from tiny fragments to twelve almost complete scrolls.

The library of scrolls was hidden in eleven caves in cliffs around Qumran. Twenty-five others show clear signs of habitation.

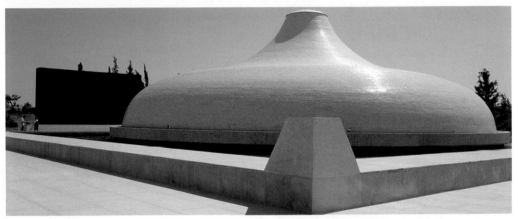

Jerusalem's Shrine of the Book houses seven, almost complete scrolls. Shaped like the lid of a scroll-jar, the white roof stands in stark contrast to the black obelisk beside it. They reflect the description given by one text of an apocalyptic battle between the forces of Good and Evil.

On a fine, spring morning in 1947, a Bedouin boy went into a cave looking for forgotten treasure - and came out with rolls of rotting leather. He had no idea that these **Dead Sea Scrolls** would provide the world's greatest insight into life in ancient Israel. The scrolls include the oldest copies of the Old Testament ever found, and show that the Bible we know today is almost identical to the one studied around the time of Jesus Christ. Some of the texts are commentaries that made the Bible relevant to their own days. These are often scathing attacks on the permissiveness of the ruling elite, or upon a world they believed had forsaken God's ways.

The texts never use the name Essenes, but refer to the Followers of the Teacher of Righteousness, or the Keepers of the

The book of Isaiah is displayed in a cabinet built like the wooden rod of a Jewish Torah scroll.

New Covenant - also translated as the New Testament. They describe a community preparing for the coming of the Messiah, who believe they are witnessing the fulfillment of all the Old Testament prophecies, who practice ritual bathing, share their wealth and conduct a daily sacred meal presided over by a priest. Many scholars see in this the roots of Christianity.

Whether written by Essenes or not, at Qumran or not, their words carry a message as clear today as it was 2,000 years ago.

Until now the spirits of truth and falsehood struggle in the hearts of men, and they walk in both wisdom and folly. According to his portion of truth so does a man hate falsehood, and according to his portion of falsehood so is he wicked and hates truth. For God has established the two spirits in equal measure until the determined end and until the Renewal.

The Community Rule - from the Dead Sea Scrolls.

These ruins of an ancient high tower date back almost 9,000 years. Modern Jericho is a mile away to the south.

Dating back almost twelve thousand years, **Jericho** claims the title of the world's oldest town. At 1200 feet (360m) below sea level, it is also the lowest.

Built around **the Spring of Elisha** that releases 1,000 gallons of water a minute, Jericho's fertile oasis in the midst of the arid Judean Desert has attracted visitors since the dawn of time.

Jericho was ancient when Joshua marched the Children of Israel into the Promised Land, but there is actually no archaeological evidence for the great battle where its *"walls came tumbling down"*, as told of in the Bible and sung of in Spirituals.

Jericho's Canaanite potters were among the best that ever worked in Palestine. This illustrated 6th century BC vase, shows how their technical expertise was matched by their sense of humor.

This face jug is just one of many finds from Jericho that can be seen in Jerusalem's Israel Museum.

Drawn by Jericho's temperate winter climate, Herod the Great built one of his most sumptuous palaces southwest of ancient Jericho, two thousand years ago. The ingenious construction on both banks of Wadi Qelt, included a large, double swimming bath.

This is said to be the sycamore that Zacchaeus climbed to see and hear Jesus, Luke 19.

Fed by one of the rare springs in the Judean wilderness, it is easy to see how the panorama of Jericho's oasis earned it the name, "the City of a Thousand Palms".

Seven centuries later, another winter palace was built in Jericho, at a site called Khirbet el-Mafjar. It was originally attributed to Hisham - the last great caliph of the Moslem Umayyad dynasty who ruled 724-743. It still carries his name - **Hisham's Palace** - although some scholars now believe it was constructed by a nephew whose one-year reign ended in his assassination. With pillared halls, two mosques and a huge royal bathhouse, the magnificent precinct was richly decorated with painted stone and plasterwork, statues and vivid mosaics. The ornamentation clearly shows the strong Byzantine influence on Islamic art and architecture at the time.

Dubbed "The Tree of Life", this is the best preserved of the palace's many fine mosaics.

This window stood within the central courtyard. Ornate stonework was often decorated with the acanthus leaf, the Islamic symbol of Paradise.

And as he went out of Jericho with his disciples and a great number of people, blind Bartimaeus, son of Timaeus, sat by the highway side begging. And when he heard it was Jesus of Nazareth, he began to cry out, and say, Jesus, thou son of David, have mercy on me. And many charged him that he should hold his peace: but he cried the more a great deal, Thou son of David, have mercy on me. ...
And Jesus answered and said unto him, What wilt thou that I should do unto thee? The blind man said unto him, Lord, that I might receive my sight. And Jesus said unto him, Go thy way; thy faith hath made thee whole. And immediately he received his sight, and followed Jesus in the way.

Mark 10:46-52.

The pillars of the Large Mosque are bathed in rose-coloured afternoon sunlight. Excavated in 1935, Hisham built, but possibly never lived in this magnificent palace.

NAZARETH

Jesus Begins His Ministry

Following His denial of the temptations of the devil, *"Jesus returned in the power of the Spirit into Galilee ... and he taught in their synagogues, being glorified of all"*, Luke 4:14-15. Eighty stone steps and column bases from Nazareth's ancient synagogue are incorporated into **the Synagogue Church**. This may be where Jesus preached or possibly a later building used by the town's first Jewish Christian community.

Jewish worship in the synagogue then, as now, consisted of prayers and readings from the Torah - the Five Books of Moses - the Prophets and the other Biblical Writings. All men were taught to read, although writing was a skill far fewer knew how to perform. Every male over thirteen years of age could be called upon to read during the Sabbath service, and men of wisdom would be invited by the rabbi to give commentary to the texts. Thus it was natural for Jesus to teach in the synagogues of the Galilee as well as to preach in the open

And he came to Nazareth, where he had been brought up: and, as his custom was, he went into the synagogue on the sabbath day, and stood up for to read. And there was delivered unto him the book of the prophet Esaias. And when he opened the book, he found the place where it was written, The Spirit of the Lord is upon me, because he hath anointed me to preach the gospel to the poor; he hath sent me to heal the brokenhearted, to preach deliverance to the captives, and recovering of sight to the blind, to set at liberty them that are bruised, to preach the acceptable year of the Lord...

Luke 4:16-21

air, as he says in John 18:20 *"I spake openly to the world; I ever taught in the synagogue, and in the temple"*.

Luke tells of the reaction that day when Jesus read from the scroll of the prophet Isaiah. At first *"all bare him witness, and wondered at the gracious words which proceeded out of his mouth"*.

A small hilltop is the site of the graceful Chapel of the Fright. Tradition says that Mary followed her son but stopped here, overcome by fear.

A cliff overlooking the Jezreel Valley is identified as the Mount of the Leap, the spot where an angry crowd wanted to cast Jesus to his death.

The Synagogue Church was built over the 6th century stone steps of Nazareth's ancient synagogue.

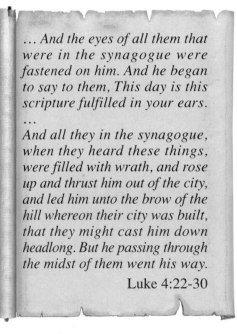

… And the eyes of all them that were in the synagogue were fastened on him. And he began to say to them, This day is this scripture fulfilled in your ears.

…

And all they in the synagogue, when they heard these things, were filled with wrath, and rose up and thrust him out of the city, and led him unto the brow of the hill whereon their city was built, that they might cast him down headlong. But he passing through the midst of them went his way.

Luke 4:22-30

But the people He had grown up among could not see beyond Jesus being the son of their local carpenter, and He said to them *"Verily I say unto you, No prophet is accepted in his own country"*. These words turned the peaceful congregation into an angry mob that drove Jesus to the edge of a precipice, ready to hurl him to his death.

The Mount of the Leap is the spot tradition identifies with the events of that day. In modern Hebrew it is called *"Har Kedumim"*, Ancient Mountain, after prehistoric remains found nearby. The ruins of an unmarked church and small monastery from the Middle Ages can be found after diligent searching.

A small hill with pine trees stands nearby. This is the site of **the Chapel of the Fright**, dedicated to the fear that Mary experienced that day.

The Sea of Galilee has many names. In his Gospel, John refers to it as the Sea of Tiberias, and it is also called Gennesaret or in Hebrew, Kinneret. This name is derived from the Hebrew word *"kinnor"* meaning harp, and relates to the Sea being shaped like a Biblical lyre. Set within the northern part of the Syrian-African Rift Valley this body of water, although called a sea, is actually a freshwater inland lake. Eight miles wide and thirteen miles long, it is fed by the Jordan River that runs in from the north.

Fish have been caught here since the dawn of time, and most of the villages along the shores drew their livelihoods from this occupation. It is no wonder that the men Jesus chose as his disciples were fishermen, or that fishing references appear in many of the parables through which he taught. One such example comes from Matthew 13:47-48, *"Again, the kingdom of heaven is like unto a net, that was cast*

Recent dry winters drove down the Sea's water level and brought to light a 2,000 year-old fishing boat. Christened the "Jesus Boat" it is displayed in the museum of Kibbutz Ginnosar.

into the sea, and gathered of every kind: Which when it was full they drew to shore, and sat down, and gathered the good into vessels, but cast the bad away". This parable carries in it the understanding of Jewish dietary laws, that permits only fish with scales and fins to be eaten. Therefore, after the catch the fishermen would have separated the permitted fish, which they kept, from the forbidden fish that they returned to the water.

A local legend tells of the dark smudge that appears on one kind of fish in the lake's waters. It is said to come from the thumb mark of the Apostle Peter, when he took a coin from a fish's mouth to pay

The Sea of Galilee. A view from Mount Arbel towards the northeast where excavations have uncovered remains of the village of Bethsaida, home to the Apostles Andrew, Peter and Philip.

Little has changed for the fishermen who cast their nets into the Sea of Galilee. They brave the same storms as the one the gospels say Jesus calmed, Matthew 8:23-26.

the temple tax, Matthew 17:27. It is called St. Peter's fish, and is one of the area's culinary delights.

The towering bluff of **Mount Arbel** dominates the lake's western shore. When Herod the Great led his Roman troops to take control of the country, the men of the Galilee fighting against him hid in caves on Arbel's cliffs. Herod ruthlessly sought them out and set fire to the caves. At its summit is the village of Arbel, which boasts a beautiful synagogue and private residence dating from Byzantine times. At the foot of the mount sits a small village now called **Migdal**. Two thousand years ago a nearby hamlet called Magdala sat at the water edge and gave its name to the lady Mary Magdalene.

All around Lake Tiberias are pleasant beaches and quiet corners. Popular are **Beit Gavriel**, at the southern shore of the

And Jesus, walking by the sea of Galilee, saw two brethren, Simon called Peter, and Andrew his brother, casting a net into the sea: for they were fishers. And he saith unto them, Follow me, and I will make you fishers of men. And straightway they left their nets, and followed him.
And going on from thence, he saw other two brethren, James the son of Zebedee, and John his brother, in a ship with Zebedee their father, mending their nets; and he called them. And they immediately left the ship and their father, and followed him.

Matthew 4:18-22

Lake, and **Kibbutz Ein Gev** on its eastern side. Both have fine restaurants. **Ein Gev, Ginnosar** and **Ramot** all boast comfortable holiday villages, making them attractive alternatives to the hotels of Tiberias as the base for a stay in the Galilee.

CAPERNAUM

Ancient Synagogue & St. Peter's house

Rejected in his hometown of Nazareth, we are told that Jesus moved to **Capernaum** and made it his own. Called Kfar Nahum in Hebrew - the village of Nahum - in its day it was one of the most important towns on the lake. Being strategically positioned on the crossroads of the region's major highways, it grew to have an estimated population of between four and five thousand.

Several important events in Jesus' life took place in Capernaum: the calling of the Disciples; the healing of Peter's mother, and others who came to their house; the healing of the Centurion's servant and the sick woman; the raising of the child from the dead; and Jesus' first confrontations with the scribes and Pharisees, Matthew 8 & 9, Mark 1 & 2, Luke 4, 7 & 8.

Some believe this synagogue may sit upon the one the gospels say was built by a Centurion.

And they went into Capernaum; and straightway on the sabbath day he entered into the synagogue; and taught. And they were astonished at his doctrine: for he taught them as one that had authority, and not as the scribes. And there was in their synagogue a man with an unclean spirit; and he cried out, saying, Let us alone; what have we to do with thee, thou Jesus of Nazareth? art thou come to destroy us? I know thee who thou art, the Holy One of God.

Mark 1:21-24.

Standing out from the black basalt houses surrounding it, Capernaum's synagogue is a sign of the town's wealth and prestige.

Images of the Ark of the Covenant and the symbol of the Menora, the seven-branched candelabrum, were found among the remains of the synagogue.

Early Jewish Christians met in private homes. St Peter's House is the best known of these church houses, or "domus ecclesiae".

When it was discovered in the last century, many thought the remains of Capernaum's dazzling synagogue were the very place where Jesus taught. However, later studies have shown that it was built at least two centuries later, although some believe it is constructed upon even older foundations.

In an area where the natural rock is volcanic black basalt, the synagogue's white limestone would have been transported to the site over a great distance, and at great public expense - testimony to the town's wealth.

The peaceful setting of this Orthodox chapel by the water's edge allows a place to reflect upon the events that took place here.

This fact is emphasized by the synagogue's decorated stonework. These are adorned with Jewish symbols, geometric designs and natural motifs from the region's flora and fauna. Originally the interior was also plastered and painted, and the wall facing Jerusalem was made especially beautiful.

The modern church erected over St. Peter's House still allows access to the ancient building.

TABGHA

The Church of the Multiplication

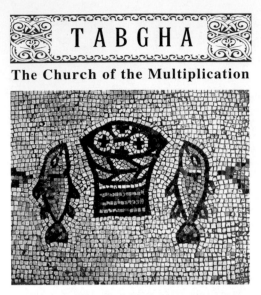

Tabgha's famous mosaic shows only four loaves in a basket. Tradition says the fifth was to be found upon the altar next to it.

And they say unto him, We have here but five loaves, and two fishes. He said, Bring them hither to me. And he commanded the multitude to sit down on the grass, and took the five loaves, and the two fishes, and looking up to heaven, he blessed, and brake, and gave the loaves to his disciples, and the disciples to the multitude. And they did all eat, and were filled: and they took up of the fragments that remained twelve baskets full. And they that had eaten were about five thousand men, beside women and children.

Matthew 14:17-21.

The Shores of the Sea of Galilee were witness to many of the great events of the Ministry of Jesus. In **Tabgha** we find **the Church of the Multiplication**, dedicated to the miracle of the multiplication of the loaves and fishes. This is recounted in all four Gospels as the feeding of the five thousand.

The church courtyard is a place of tranquility for visiting pilgrims.

A modern church was recently erected over the exact lines of the fifth century chapel that stood here until it was destroyed by the Persians in 614. Inside its halls it preserves one of the country's most exquisite mosaic pavements, depicting some of the many birds and flowers found at the lakeside. By the church's altar is the famous image of the loaves and the fishes.

The name Tabgha itself derives from an Arabic mispronunciation of the Greek word *"Heptapegon"*, meaning the seven springs. In 384, Egeria, a visiting pilgrim nun, described the site in these words

"Not far away from Capernaum are some stone steps where the Lord stood. And in the same place by the sea is a grassy field with plenty of hay and many palm trees. By them are seven springs, each flowing strongly. And this is the field where the Lord fed the people with the five loaves and the two fishes. In fact the stone on which the Lord placed the bread has now been made into an altar". A simple altar now stands above that stone.

Also found in Tabgha are ruins of a chapel that recalls the Sermon on the Mount, and **the Chapel of the Primacy** (pages 158/9) that commemorates Christ's Resurrection.

Detail of the mid-5th century mosaic pavement.

Careful construction has preserved one of the country's artistic masterpieces.

Chorazim was an important town at the time of Jesus.

Byzantine-style stonework from the ancient synagogue.

> Then he began to upbraid the cities wherein most of his mighty works were done, because they repented not: Woe unto thee, Chorazim! Woe unto thee, Bethsaida! For if the mighty works, which were done in you, had been done in Tyre and Sidon, they would have repented long ago in sackcloth and ashes.
>
> Matthew 11:20-21

Chorazim

Jesus cursed the towns of **Chorazim**, Bethsaida and Capernaum for their disbelief and by the 4th century Chorazim was in ruins. Among the remains of its ancient synagogue archaeologists found an armed seat carved out of a single basalt rock. This is thought by many to be an example of *"the seat of Moses"*, the inscribed bench of a local teacher, referred to in Matthew 23:2.

Gamala

On the Lake's eastern shore, **Gamala** was a Zealot city. Ultra-nationalists with fervent Messianic beliefs, the Zealots led the ill-fated revolt against Rome in 67 AD. At Gamala they mounted the last Galilean stand against Vespasian's army. For days they beat back waves of attacks. Then the Romans breached the walls and began a systematic slaughter of men, women and children. The last defenders threw themselves to their deaths rather than fall into Roman hands. Thousands died. Only two women survived.

The synagogue of Gamala is one of the oldest in the country.

Like the hump of a camel, Gamala took its name from the hill's shape.

Pilgrims have long been drawn to visit the site of Jesus' first public miracle. It took place in the Galilee village of **Cana** - now called Kefar Kana - just outside Nazareth. Many describe how they drank from the same pure water that Jesus had turned into wine, at the spring to the west of the town.

Excavations unearthed an ancient synagogue, and a later courtyard and mosaic pavement. These show that Cana was a thriving town two thousand years ago. It may be that an early Judeo-Christian community lived here soon after Jesus'

The Franciscan church was erected over ruins of a 6th century sanctuary.

Jars in both churches are designed like the ones used in the miracle.

lifetime, perhaps sharing the synagogue as a place of worship until they constructed a church of their own.

Later, the Byzantines and the Crusaders built churches here. In 1551 a Greek Orthodox church was erected, replaced in 1886 by the one seen today. The present Franciscan church, completed in 1881, is built over the remains of Cana's earliest site of veneration.

When the ruler of the feast had tasted the water that was made wine, and knew not whence it was: ... the governor of the feast called the bridegroom, and saith unto him, Every man at the beginning doth set forth good wine; and when men have well drunk, then that which is worse: but thou hast kept the good wine until now. This beginning of miracles did Jesus in Cana of Galilee, and manifested forth his glory.

John 2:7-11

Two churches recall Jesus' first miracle performed here, one is Franciscan (left), and the other is Greek Orthodox (right).

KURSI

Although Jesus spent most of his time among the Jews, he did sometimes minister further afield. On one occasion he crossed the Sea of Galilee to visit Kursi, referred to as Gadarenes or Garasenes in the Gospels. It was here that he drove many devils out of a man possessed (two men according to Matthew). Afterwards the townspeople begged him to leave.

In Byzantine times a village called Korsia flourished here, and a large monastery and church were erected. Decorated with flora and fauna mosaics, one shows the local swine.

And there was a good way off from them an herd of many swine feeding. So the devils besought him, saying, If thou cast us out, suffer us to go away into the herd of swine. And he said to them, Go. And when they were come out, they went into the herd of swine: and, behold, the whole herd of swine ran violently down a steep place into the sea, and perished in the waters.
Matthew 8:29-32

A visitor to the Galilee in the last century described his sojourn thus, *"There is no journey in all the world to be compared with this, none of such sweet memories, not even in the Holy Land"*.

A beautiful black basalt Byzantine monastery marks the traditional spot where Jesus exorcised the demons into a herd of swine.

TIBERIAS

Built by the son of Herod the Great, Herod Antipas, who ruled from 4 BC to 39 AD, **Tiberias** was named after of the Roman Caesar, Tiberius. While constructing the sparkling new metropolis an ancient cemetery was uncovered. Observant Jews refused to live there, but still it grew to become the main city of the Sea of Galilee.

Today Tiberias is a centre for tourism, with a wide range of hotels and an abundance of restaurants to suite all tastes. Especially attractive are those on the lakeside promenade. Afterwards one can embark on a trip around the Lake aboard a ship styled after the large fishing vessels of antiquity. Also on the promenade, is the Galilee Experience, a sound-and-light show on the history of the Galilee. Near the northern end of the promenade are the ruins of the Crusader castle of Tiberias

The hot springs of Hammat Tiberias are still active, just outside the town.
Its synagogue's 4th century mosaic combines religious and astrological symbols.

The city of Tiberias was founded around 19 AD by Herod Antipas, ruler of the Galilee in the time of Jesus.

that was besieged by Saladin prior to the Battle of Hittin, mentioned in the text on Sepphoris (Pages 48/9).

Not to be missed are the hot springs of **Hammat Tiberias**, in the south of the town. At a constant 60 degrees centigrade (140° F), travelers have been drawn to these medicinal spas for over two millennia. In the Middle Ages the great Moroccan traveler Ibn Battuta recorded his visit in these words, *"I then went to the town of Tabariah. It was once a large and important town, but now there are only a few simple remains, which however show its past grandeur and importance. There you will find marvellous baths which have two separate quarters, one for men and the other for women. The water in these baths is very warm"*.

One hundred meters south of Hammat Tiberias, on the banks of the lake, the remains of **the Synagogue of Severus** were found. Its magnificent Byzantine mosaic shows the most sacred Jewish symbol, Jerusalem's Temple where the Ark of the Covenant was kept, above the twelve signs of the zodiac with Helios, the sun god, at its center.

The hot baths of Hammat Gader outside Tiberias were rated among the best in the Roman Empire. Today a nearby alligator park attracts visitors as well.

Further afield beneath the slopes of the Golan Heights, are the hot springs of **Hammat Gader**. Also rich in healing properties, their reputation spread throughout the Roman world and lasted well into the Byzantine age, as the ruins of extensive construction show.

THE MOUNT OF THE BEATITUDES

Sunshine lights the eight stained glass windows that proclaim the words of the Beatitudes.

Above the lake not far from Capernaum, is a tree-lined hill known as **the Mount of the Beatitudes**. This is where tradition places the spot Jesus delivered the Sermon on the Mount.

This concentrated teaching included Jesus showing the disciples how to pray (the Lord's Prayer), many lessons in the form of parables for them and the multitudes, and the eight verses known as the Beatitudes. Together they have been described as the Keynote of the New Age Jesus came to introduce.

Built by the Order of St. Francis, the arched ambulatory of the octagonal church gives a splendid view of Lake Tiberias.

And seeing the multitudes, he went up into a mountain: and when he was set, his disciples came unto him: and he opened his mouth, and taught them, saying,

Blessed are the poor in spirit: for theirs is the kingdom of heaven. Blessed are they that mourn: for they shall be comforted. Blessed are the meek: for they shall inherit the earth. Blessed are they which do hunger and thirst after righteousness: for they shall be filled. Blessed are the merciful: for they shall obtain mercy. Blessed are the pure in heart: for they shall see God. Blessed are the peacemakers: for they shall be called the children of God. Blessed are they that are persecuted for righteousness' sake: for theirs is the kingdom of heaven.

Blessed are ye, when men shall revile you, and persecute you, and shall say all manner of evil against you falsely, for my sake. Rejoice, and be exceeding glad: for great is your reward in heaven: for so persecuted they the prophets which were before you. Ye are the salt of the earth … Ye are the light of the world.

Matthew 5:1-14

Built in the 1930's, the Church of the Beatitudes is set in one of the most beautiful gardens in the land.

On a summit overlooking the Sea of Galilee, a domed octagonal church reminds visitors of Jesus' eight Beatitudes.

BETH SHEAN

Beth Shean belonged to a league of ten cities referred to in the New Testament as the Decapolis. These were situated in the northern part of the Jordan Valley and in Transjordan, and the Gospels use the name equally for the towns and for the whole region. We are told that when Jesus told the man exorcised of devils to *"Go home to thy friends, and tell them how great things the Lord hath done for thee, …*

The city existed through Roman, Byzantine and early Arab times. It was eventually destroyed in 794 AD.

(And) he departed, and began to publish in Decapolis how great things Jesus had done", Mark 5:19-20.

Beth Shean was an important town in Biblical times. King Saul's decapitated

And his fame went throughout all Syria: … and there followed him great multitudes of people from Galilee, and from Decapolis, and from Jerusalem, and from Judea, and from beyond the Jordan.

Matthew 4:24-25

body was hung on its walls after his defeat at the hands of the Philistines (1 Samuel 31). The city grew to prominence during the reign of King Solomon who rebuilt its great walls. The high tel or mound dates from this time, and excavations revealed a wealth of finds and information from the period.

After the conquest of Alexander the Great in 333 BC, Beth Shean was renamed Scythopolis in honour of the mercenaries who came from Scythia, by the Black Sea. Together with the other cities of the Decapolis, Beth Shean became an important centre of Hellenistic culture. Later, the cities flourished under Rome which granted them special status. They were allowed to mint their own coins and had a rare degree of autonomy. Beth Shean's large theater and its many fine mosaics are evidence of how much the city prospered during this time.

Built around 200 AD, Beth Shean's impressive amphitheater seated over 5,000 spectators. The Biblical Tel is clearly visible beyond.

MOUNT GILBOA

Jesus' journeys from the Galilee would have taken him through the **Jezreel Valley** before entering Samaria where he healed the ten lepers - though only one *"turned back, and with a loud voice glorified God"*.

As he went to Jerusalem,... he passed through the midst of Samaria and Galilee. And as he entered into a certain village, there met him ten men that were lepers, ... he said unto them, Go shew yourselves unto the priests. And ... as they went, they were cleansed.

Luke 17:11-14

Mount Gilboa looks out over the fertile Jezreel Valley.

He may have rested on route like other travelers, by the lush pools of the **Sachne** or the springs of Ein Harod by the foot of the forested **Mount Gilboa**. This was the site of the selection of Gideon's army, spoken of in the Book of Judges 7. Mount Gilboa is still a favorite spot for visitors especially during the springtime when the earth is a carpet of multi-coloured wildflowers.

The Sachne's natural pool is popular during the hot summer months.

BANYAS

At the foot of Mount Hermon, in the north of the Galilee, the spring of **the Banyas** flows out of a cave. Joining the River Jordan, its waters descend 1700 feet (510m) to feed the Sea of Galilee.

In ancient times many springs were held to be sacred - especially those like Banyas that emerged from the mouth of a cave. The Greeks settled here and built a temple dedicated to Zeus. They named the place Paneas after Pan, the god of shepherds and nature. Banyas is the Arabic pronunciation of that name.

When Jesus came into the coasts of Caesaria Philippi, he asked his disciples, saying, Whom do men say that I the Son of man am? And they said, Some say that thou art John the Baptist: some, Elias; some Jeremias, or one of the prophets. He said unto them, But whom say ye that I am? And Simon Peter answered and said, Thou art the Christ, the Son of the living God.

Matthew 16:13-16

Herod the Great erected a temple to Caesar Augustus in the town. His son Philip made it the capital of his tetrarchy, and renamed it Caesaria. Thus it became known in the Gospels as Caesaria Philippi. It was here that Jesus brought the disciples; here that Jesus said, *"Thou art Peter and upon this rock I will build my church; and the gates of hell shall not prevail against it"*, Matthew 16:18.

The waterfall of Banyas draws visitors all year round.

Cut out of the rock, these Romans niches once housed statues of the god Pan.

MOUNT HERMON

After the episode at Banyas, Jesus went to a high mountain where he was transfigured. Although none of the Gospels say where this occurred, one tradition holds that it was on nearby **Mount Hermon**, the highest peak in the Near East. Most, however, prefer to place the event at Mount Tabor (see pages 78-9).

And after six days Jesus taketh with him Peter and James and John, and leadeth them up into an high mountain apart by themselves: and he was transfigured before them.

Mark 9:2

Called the Sarion in Biblical times, the Hermon is actually not one mountain but an eighteen-and-a-half-mile long chain of peaks, the highest reaching over 9,200 feet (2,790m). For almost half the year its summit can be seen from up to 60 miles away and is usually covered with snow. The snow provides one third of the country's drinking water - and all its skiing.

In a land better known for its heat, the snows of the Hermon are a magnet for winter visitors.

Mount Hermon is seen by one tradition as the site of the Transfiguration.

NIMROD'S CASTLE

Perched on a lonely hilltop, the Castle of Nimrod watches over the fertile valley of the Upper Galilee.

Legend claims **the Castle of Nimrod** was built by the king of Babel, son of Cam *"the first to hold power above the earth"*. Indeed, remains of fortification at this obviously strategic position date far back into antiquity. Yet most of its fame - and almost all its construction - spring from the period of the Crusades.

At that time it constantly changed hands between the Arabs and the Frankish knights. On one rare occasion the Christians even fought together with soldiers from Damascus to oust the Emir of Banyas from his fortress. When the Crusaders themselves were driven out, the castle became a shrine of the *"Hashashin"*. These mystic Shi'ite Moslems practiced political murder - and gave the world the word, Assassin.

Not far from Nimrod, nestling on the eastern foothills of Mount Hermon, is the quiet Druze village of **Majdal Shams**.

Meaning the Tower of the Sun, the town is now peaceful, although the Druze have a proud military heritage. They successfully fought the French at the turn of the last century. A statue of their hero, Sultan el-Atrach, dominates the town square.

MOUNT TABOR

Basilica of the Transfiguration

The mosaic shows Christ transfigured, with Moses holding the tablets of the Law on the left, and Elijah on the right.

Mount Tabor is where ancient Christian traditions place the miracle of the Transfiguration of Christ. Rising suddenly 1,500 feet (450m) above the Biblical Plain of Esdraelon, Tabor has been ascribed with sacred quality since the time of the Phoenicians. Known also as the Holy Mountain, the Biblical Psalmist called on it and Mount Hermon to witness the glory of the Lord, *"Tabor and Hermon shall rejoice in thy name"* Psalm 89:12.

In the 4th century the first **Basilica of the Transfiguration** was erected at the summit, and five hundred years later it hosted four churches, a bishopric and at least 18 monks. The Crusaders enlarged the Basilica and also built an Abbey with fortified walls to withstand Moslem attacks. Eventually however, all of Tabor's churches were destroyed.

The present Basilica was raised in 1924. It was designed in a grand medieval style, befitting the sanctity of its situation that was described in these words, *"Tabor rises up to Heaven like an altar that the Creator built to himself"*. Indeed, when you look out upon the Holy Land from Mount Tabor you can feel the panorama of history and faith stretched out before you.

The modern Basilica captures the majesty felt on the Mount.

*The Greek Orthodox chapel is
dedicated to the prophet Elijah.*

*And (He) was transfigured before
them: and his face did shine like
the sun, and his raiment was white
as the light. And, behold, there
appeared unto them Moses and
Elias talking with him. ... behold,
a bright cloud overshadowed
them: and behold a voice out of
the cloud, which said, This is my
beloved Son, in whom I am well
pleased.*

Matthew 17:2-5.

*Mount Tabor stands out gracefully
above the Jezreel Valley.*

Beth Shearim - House of Gates - was an important Jewish center following the destruction of the Temple in Jerusalem in the 1st century AD. It was home to Rabbi Jehuda HaNasi who presided over of the Sanhedrin, before he moved this Rabbinical Court to Sepphoris (pages 48/9). He is known to have been buried here, and the tomb of his two sons was found during recent excavations of the large necropolis.

All three were descendents of Rabban Gamaliel the Elder, the great Jewish thinker and leading Pharisee of his day. He was

Under pleasant wooded hills, Beth Shearim is a gateway into the past. It once was the central cemetery for the whole Jewish world.

Beth Shearim's necropolis (city of the dead) is a labyrinth of catacombs carved into the hillside.

a teacher of St. Paul. This we know from Paul's own words, spoken to an assembled crowd by the Temple steps, *"I am verily a man which am a Jew, born in Tarsus, a city in Cilicia, yet brought up in this city at the feet of Gamaliel, and taught according to the perfect manner of the law of the fathers"*, Acts 22:3.

In all, thirty-one burial chambers were found carved deep into the hillside. The central hall of the largest chamber is 160 feet long (50m) and its complex contained over 130 stone coffins. Some of them are as much as nine feet (3m) long, and weigh 5 tons. Beth Shearim's *"City of the Dead"* is unique in all Israel.

Notables from as far away as Mesopotamia, Southern Arabia and Phoenicia were buried in Beth Shearim.

SAMARIA

In the center of the country, separating the Galilee from Judea, lie the rolling hills of **Samaria**. Two thousand years ago the region was thickly forested > oaks, carobs and pistachio trees growing out of lush bushes of myrtle, broom and acanthus. Today most of the hills are terraced with olive groves and vines, or stripped down to low undergrowth and bare rock.

Though Jesus often passed through the region of Samaria on his way to and from Jerusalem, it is hardly mentioned in the Gospels, and nothing is said of its hilltop city, also called Samaria. This was the capital of the ancient kingdom of Israel established in 876 BC by the Biblical king, Omri.

Destroyed in the 3rd century by Alexander the Great, Samaria was later occupied by the Romans who gave the city to Herod the Great. Herod rebuilt the town, calling it **Sebaste**, Greek for Augustus, in honour of the first Roman Emperor of the same name. It was a magnificent place, the upper town with an Acropolis and Royal Palace where archaeologists unearthed one of the finest collections of ivory carvings. The lower section

These ruins are all that's left of the Greek tower once called "the finest monument in all the land".

was dominated by the huge Forum with high columns and carved capitals. In his typical paranoia, Herod surrounded the whole town with a double wall, 52 feet thick (15m).

The traditional site of **the Tomb of John the Baptist** is also found in Samaria, which made it a place of pilgrimage from early in the Christian era. As elsewhere, the tomb is built over an ancient cave where the prophets Elisha and Obadiah supposedly lie. Some traditions say that Elizabeth and Zachariah, John's parents, are also buried there. In the 1150's the Crusaders built a church on the spot that was said to be the loveliest in the land.

Remains of the Forum of the city Herod renamed Sebaste.

THE SAMARITANS

Only about seven hundred souls remain today of a people that was one million strong when Jesus told the parable of the **Good Samaritan**, Luke 10:30. Making a Samaritan the *"good neighbour"* was a blow to Jewish pride as Jews had spurned the sect for generations. The sect were occupying Assyrians who had intermarried with Israelites in the 7th century BC, and adopted Mosaic law. Rejected because of their pagan roots, they were barred from helping rebuild the Temple in Jerusalem when the Jews returned from exile in Babylonia. Eventually they built their own temple on **Mount Gerizim** near Nablus, and prospered. By 36 AD they had grown powerful enough to demand an end to the 18 year rule of the hated Pontius Pilate - but only after hundreds had been massacred at the foot of Mount Gerizim by order of the Roman procurator.

Every spring Samaritans gather to celebrate the Passover exactly as it is written in the book of Exodus - including sacrificing the paschal lamb.

Different from Hebrew, Arabic and Aramiac, the Samaritans' Torah scrolls are written in their own unique script.

Mount Gerizim is where most of them live today, still practicing their own unique customs. They accept only the Five Books of Moses as sacred (the first five books of the Bible), Moses as God's only prophet, and Mount Gerizim as His sanctuary. They read the Ten Commandments as nine to which they added a tenth of their own - the uniqueness of Mount Gerizim. At Passover all the Samaritan families gather for 40 days and nights at the top of their sacred mount where their High Priest recites the story of the Exodus to the whole community.

Samaritans pray on Mount Gerizim where they say Abraham took Isaac to be sacrificed.

JACOB'S WELL - NABLUS

The Gospel of John tells of the meeting between Jesus and a woman of the Samaritans that takes place at **Jacob's Well** in the city of Sychar, while Jesus was travelling from Judea back to the Galilee. He speaks to the Samaritan despite the deep rift between their two peoples, offering everlasting life to the woman - and through her to all the peoples of the world.

Since Early Christian times the location of this event has been placed in the Biblical town **Shechem**. Known as Jabal Batin in Arabic, it's more commonly called **Nablus** by the west, from the name Neapolis, given to it by the Roman Titus in 72 AD. The Byzantines raised a church here in the 4th century, and today a Greek Orthodox monastery stands over the ruins of the church and the well.

Jacob's Well drops to a depth of about 115 feet (35m).

> *But whosoever drinketh of the water that I shall give him shall never thirst; but the water that I shall give him shall be in him a well of water springing up into everlasting life.*
>
> John 4:14

Also fascinating to visit are the many traditional crafts workshops. Nablus is famous for the many factories that produce soap from olive oil and soda by methods used for millennia.

ST. GEORGE'S MONASTERY

Destroyed after the Crusades, St. George's was thoroughly rebuilt in the last century.

Jesus told the parable of the Good Samaritan in response to the questions of a smart lawyer who asked what he needed to do to attain eternal life. Seeing he was an educated man, Jesus asked him what the scriptures say. He replied quoting the core Jewish prayer recited daily from Deuteronomy 6:5 *"Thou shalt love the Lord thy God with all thine heart, with all thy soul and with all thy might,"* and added to it a saying of the great teacher, Rabbi Hillel, *"Love thy neighbour as thyself"*. Jesus confirmed that this was in truth the way. But the lawyer was not satisfied, demanding to know of Jesus, Who is my neighbour? To which he surely received an answer he did not expect.

The road from Jerusalem to Jericho traditionally wound the length of **Wadi Qelt**, a perilous and winding desert path. In places one can still see the remains of the Roman road that followed the same course. Off the road near the spring of Ain el Qelt one comes suddenly upon **the Monastery of St George of Koziba**.

As if pinned to the face of the cliff, St George's is one of the country's most picturesque monasteries.

Built into the cliff over a picturesque gorge, St George's was founded in 420 by five Syrian hermits living in a small cave. A century later monks had erected a fifty-foot bell tower, domed chapel and small rooms around an open courtyard. These had all been destroyed and rebuilt by the turn of the first millennium when it was thoroughly restored by the Crusaders. The monastery one now sees was constructed at the beginning of the last century, but hermits still occupy some of the caves along the wadi.

Farming the terraced slopes kept the monastery self-sufficient for generations.

"A certain man went down from Jerusalem to Jericho, and fell among thieves, which stripped him of his raiment, and wounded him, and departed, leaving him half dead. And by chance there came down a certain priest that way: and when he saw him, he passed by on the other side. And likewise a Levite, when he was at the place, came and looked on him, and passed by on the other side.

But a certain Samaritan, as he journeyed, came where he was: and when he saw him, he had compassion on him, and went to him, and bound up his wounds, pouring in oil and wine, and set him on his own beast, and brought him to an inn, and took care of him. And on the morrow when he departed, he took out two pence, and gave them to the host, and said unto him, Take care of him; and whatever thou spendeth more, when I come again, I will repay thee".

Luke 10:30-35

At 1,350 feet (411m) below sea level, **the Dead Sea** is the lowest point on the surface of the world (cf California's Death Valley 85.5m). Called the Salt Sea in the Old Testament, this is the basin of the northern section of the Great Rift Valley that begins in Syria and eventually reaches Kenya and Tanzania in Central Africa.

The lake is 31 miles (50 km) long, 11 miles (17km) wide and 1,380 feet (420m) deep. With high atmospheric pressure and high temperatures all year round, the sea evaporates very fast. Although it is constantly fed by fresh water from the Jordan River and the nearby springs like those at **Ein Feshkha**, the evaporation is such that the Dead Sea has a salt content of over 30% - more than 10 times saltier than the Mediterranean Sea.

The sun was risen upon the earth when Lot entered into Zo'ar. Then the Lord rained upon Sodom and upon Gomorrah brimstone and fire from the Lord out of heaven; and he overthrew those cities, ... But his wife looked back from behind him, and she became a pillar of salt.

Genesis 19:23-26

The salts are actually a mixture of many minerals so dense that they keep a person afloat. Called the Dead Sea because it used to be thought that no life at all existed in

Ein Bokek's health spas treat visitors to breathtaking views and invigorating mud baths.

its water, it is now known that there is a wealth of micro-organisms that find the Dead Sea's unique ecosystem an attractive home. The mineral rich waters have also been attracting humans for generations, both for its therapeutic waters and mud baths, and just to wonder at the constantly changing colors of its majestic - and often eerie - landscape.

At many places on the road around the Sea, especially in the area of **Ein Bokek**, signposts point to bathing areas. It is always best to bathe at one of these organized sites, as it is advised to wash off the high salt content of the water. Also found here is the international center for the treatment of psoriasis. Further inland, a short drive brings

The multi-colored Dead Sea with the Mountains of Moab in the background.

One only needs to look at the landscape to understand the story of Lot's wife being turned to a pillar of salt.

you to **Wadi Bokek**. Less visited than Ein Gedi, this lush oasis set among gorges is not to be missed.

Across the lake are the Mountains of Moab, while to the west are the mountains of the Judean Desert. Southward is **Sodom**, center of the mineral industry in an area of strange salt formations. These bring to mind the story of Sodom and Gomorrah, and how Lots wife was turned to a pillar of salt.

Six miles north of Sodom is the spa of kibbutz **Neve Zohar**. Its hot sulphur springs have been famous for centuries and the history of the therapeutic uses of the lake is attractively traced in the small museum.

Because of its high salt content it really is impossible to sink in the Dead Sea.

EIN GEDI

In contrast to the stark landscape of the surrounding Judean Desert, the **Ein Gedi National Park** is a luxuriant paradise of semi-tropical vegetation. Fed by a brook that rises at **Ein Gedi** itself - the Spring of the Young Goat - the waters of Nahal David and Nahal Arugot (about a mile to the south) cascade down the mountainside overlooking the Dead Sea.

Evidence of human occupation here dates back to the third millennium BC - testimony to the area's attraction throughout the ages.

My beloved is unto me as a cluster of camphire in the vineyards of Engedi. Behold thou art fair, my love; behold thou art fair; thou hast doves eyes. Behold thou art fair, my beloved, yea pleasant: Also our bed is green. The beams of our house are cedar, and our rafters are fir.

Song of Solomon 1:14-17

According to the Old Testament the young David fled to these hills to hide from the wrath of King Saul, (1 Samuel 24), and here, in the time of King Solomon, a great perfume industry blossomed. Later, the Romans built a bathhouse at the spring, and in Byzantine times a synagogue was erected nearby. Its beautiful mosaic floor is still visible almost completely intact.

Ein Gedi's nature reserve is brimming with wildlife - flora and fauna. As well as Nubian ibex, it is common to see whole colonies of Rock Hyrax sunning themselves on the boulders - or scuttling away when they've been disturbed. Much less common is a sight of the Negev Leopard. Not dangerous to man, several pairs of these small leopards live in the hills around Ein Gedi, but a glimpse is rare, as they are nocturnal hunters, resting during the hot hours of the day.

Ein Gedi's main waterfall drops from a height of almost 600 feet.

The canyons of Nahal David and Nahal Arugot are great places for short or long hikes all year round.

The Nature Reserve has a field school and hostel, while **Kibbutz Ein Gedi** boasts a high standard guest house/hotel.

More information about the area, and arrangements for exploring the desert by foot or by jeep, can be obtained at the Metzokeh Dragot Information Center, situated close to nearby **Kibbutz Mitzpeh Shalem**. This kibbutz - a pioneer of winter crop cultivation - has some of the best date orchards in the country, and also a modern factory for cosmetics based on the natural ingredients from the Dead Sea. The kibbutz also offers reasonably priced lodgings.

Ein Gedi is home to several herds of impressive Nubian ibex - wild mountain goats.

MASADA

Towering 1,300 feet above the shores of the Dead Sea, the palace at the natural fortress of **Masada** was originally constructed by the Hasmonean king, Alexander Jannaeus - but that was completely rebuilt by Herod the Great. Ever fearful of a revolt against him, and of Cleopatra's dream of rebuilding the Egyptian Empire that once included Judea, Herod made the almost inaccessible mountaintop his fortified refuge in case he ever needed a safe retreat.

These cosmetic and perfume utensils were discovered in the bathhouse.

Around Masada's summit Herod created a casement wall strengthened by watchtowers. He cut two extensive systems of cisterns into the rock to provide water in time of siege. These held over 40,000 cubic meters of water, all of which had to be carried up Masada's winding paths by hand. Herod crowned Masada with two sumptuous palaces furnished with every conceivable luxury to while away the time. However, although he never used Masada's massive defenses, its fortifications were put to the test just a generation later.

Masada boasts three bathhouses - two private baths for Herod, and this public bathhouse for visitors.

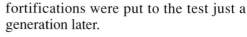

This pair of 1st century sandals probably belonged to one of the Zealots who held Masada during the Revolt against Rome.

After the fall of Jerusalem in 70 AD, the last remnants of Jewish resistance to Rome fled to the desert stronghold of Masada. Less than a thousand defenders called Zealots, or *Sicarii*, held out for three years against a siege of over 10,000 well-equipped, battle hardened soldiers. In the end the Romans built a huge wedge-shaped ramp rising to Masada's summit.Under the protection of an ironclad tower erected on a stone platform at the ramp's top, the Romans pounded Masada's wall with a battering ram. When it collapsed they found another, wooden wall that they set ablaze.

Herod built his Hanging Palace on three levels of Masada's northern precipice.

Seeing their defenses crumble, the Zealots inside chose mass suicide rather than life as slaves or death for Roman sport in one of the amphitheaters. After three years, the Roman Legionnaires broke into Masada only to find 960 corpses of men, women and children who had died in freedom. Two old women and five children survived to tell the world the tale, one that has become a symbol of the spirit of modern Israel.

The site of Masada is open to the public from 06.30 until 16.00. The cable car begins operating at 08.00.

Today, Masada's summit can be reached by two ancient footpaths or by modern cable car.

CAESAREA

A massive moat surrounds the Crusader citadel.

In 40 BC, the Roman senate pronounced Herod king of Judea - making him just another one of Rome's many client kings. But Herod was a man of great vision who wanted nothing less than to copy Rome's glory in this tiny Jewish country. To that end Herod embarked on an extensive building program unparalleled in the known world.

Herod constructed huge fortified palaces, great temples, amphitheaters and aqueducts - but by far his most ambitious project was the creation of a brand new port city he called **Caesarea** in honor of his Roman masters. On the Mediterranean coast, half way between modern Tel Aviv and Haifa, the city arose dressed with all the splendor Herod could muster. It had a temple dedicated to his mentor, Caesar Augustus, an amphitheater, theater, hippodrome and baths - all clad in imported white marble.

Since Caesarea has no springs, Herod built an aqueduct stretching over nine miles to supply the city.

Meanwhile, despite all the difficulties they encountered, Herod's engineers performed near miracles constructing the harbor. They employed underwater concrete casting centuries ahead of its time, and even created a unique sluicing system that periodically flushed the harbor to prevent a build up of sand: a problem that continued to plague all other Mediterranean ports for generations. In just over a decade they had built the largest artificial harbor in the ancient world.

Still standing after two thousand years, the arches of Caesarea's limestone aqueduct catch the rays of the setting sun.

Unfortunately, the site Herod had chosen for his new maritime center was not only lacking even a natural bay - but he had placed it on an unstable fault of the Mediterranean shore. As soon as it was finished, the harbor of Caesarea began to sink. Today, most of what remains is buried under sand beneath the water.

In 6 AD Rome annexed Judea, and Caesarea became the seat of the Roman governor. The only archaeological evidence of Pontius Pilate came to light here recently when his name was found carved in stone.

Caesarea appears in the New Testament, in the book of the Acts of the Apostles. This tells of Philip the Deacon who ministered here, Acts 8:40; of Simon Peter who converted Cornelius the Centurion - making him the first Gentile to adopt Christianity, Acts 10; and of Paul who was imprisoned while waiting to be sent to Rome for trial, Acts 25. Twice more Caesarea saw tragedy when its stadium became the stage for the massacres of thousands of Jews who took part in the revolts against Rome.

Extensive remains of Herod's 370 acre city, as well as the ruins of the later Crusader citadel, can be seen at Caesarea's impressive excavations - the largest in the Holy Land - and in the Museum of **Caesarea Antiquities** at nearby **Kibbutz Sdot Yam**.

With the ocean as a backdrop, Caesarea's Roman theater still holds concerts for up to 5,000 spectators.

In this red porphyry statue some see Caesar Hadrian who put down the great Jewish revolt of 132 AD.

Intricate carvings once adorned every surface of the city's public buildings.

93

ACRE

Tracing its roots back over 4,000 years, **Acre**, Akko in the Bible, is one of the oldest-running seaports in the world. Its name was first recorded when the expanding Egyptian Empire conquered it in the 15th century BC. Growing as a trading center when Phoenician mariners were masters of the seas, Akko exploited its strategic position on the famous Via Maris - the Way of the Sea. By then its glass industry was so important that one ancient historian even claimed that glass was invented here.

Unmentioned by the Gospels, St. Paul passed through the city on his travels and speaks of it in Acts 21:7. by its Greek name, Ptolemais.

On a spring afternoon, Roberts' first view of Acre backed by the brilliant blue Mediterranean was enough to inspire his artistic imagination. It was, he noted in his journal, "a picture which would have satisfied Turner himself".

The Khan el-Umdan, Inn of the Columns, was erected in 1906 by the Ottoman Sultan Abdul Hammid as a hotel for travelling merchants.

Acre then disappears in history until the Crusades, when the legendary King Richard the Lion-heart captured the city, in 1191. From that time it was called St. Jean d'Acre, after the Knights of St. John who made it their headquarters. Following the fall of Jerusalem, Acre became the capital of the Latin Kingdom, growing into one of the greatest ports in Christendom, until 1291 when the Mameluks razed it to the ground.

Acre's restored **Crusader Citadel** is part of a city that once housed 50,000 inhabitants - it is among the best examples of underground architecture in the country. Its many passageways run down to the port or to the winding alleys of **the Souk**. It is worth taking the time to wander through Acre, visiting **the Khan el-Umdan** and **the Al Jazzar mosque**, discovering history as you go, and relaxing over fresh caught seafood or a Middle Eastern vegetarian meal - specialities of the port.

In 1781 Al Jazzar, "the Butcher of Akko", successfully held off Napoleon's army by threatening to execute any soldier who retreated. In thanks to Allah he erected the mosque that bears his name.

Acre's port holds 4,000 years of history - and a wealth of Middle Eastern hospitality.

Life in Jesus' Time

The Yearly Cycle

Passover

Purim

Hanukkah

Like many cultures of ancient origin, the Jewish people follow a lunar calendar. Watching the monthly waxing and waning of our nearest heavenly neighbor, the year begins with the appearance of a new moon and the

Shavuot

Rosh Hashana

Purim

Adar

March

Passover

Nisan

Aprild

Iyyar

May

Sivan

Tammuz

June

Av

July

ugust

Yom Kippur

celebration of two major festivals coincide with the rising of the full moon. Some Jewish festivals commemorate events in the nation's history while others mark the passage of the yearly agricultural cycle in this part of the world.

Succoth

Domestic Life

Throughout the ages the family stood at the very heart of Jewish society. The father was the undisputed head of his family while the mother preserved the Jewish line

itself - a balance that gave society strength and endurance. Women were responsible for running the home in which several generations would live, eat and sleep together. Most homes had only very basic furniture, except for the houses of the rich who lived mainly in the big towns and cities.

Stone motars would be use to grind grain into flour – t country's staple diet.

Typical examples of the simple oil lamps that lit homes.

Simple clay was used for storage jars and cooking pots.

Wood and earthenware plate were more commonly used by village folk.

Stone table and storage jar. Stone and glassware were preferred by the rich. As non-absorbent materials they did not require ritual cleansing.

Herod the Great was allowed to mint bronze coins, but not ones of gold or silver. Pontius Pilate later upset the status quo and offended the Jews by printing Roman symbols on his coins.

Eastern women have always loved jewelry made from precious metals and multi-colored stones. This jewelry case slides open from the bottom.

A mirror made of metal set in wood.

All but the most religious Jews probably wore the standard dress of the eastern Roman Empire.

A draw-string purse and leather wallet were found at Ein Gedi.

Remains of knee-length two-piece tunics with double stripes like these were found at Ein Gedi and Masada. Both men and women would also have worn woolen cloaks.

These simple sandals were typical of the time.

The women of the region had started using cosmetics long before to enhance their beauty. Perfumes and oils were kept in glass or clay phials, powder in wooden boxes. Eye shadow was applied with bronze sticks.

This bone comb was found among the Zealot remains at Masada.

Life in Jesus' Time

Crafts

Groups of houses like these may have been typical of villages 2,000 years ago. Called *"insulae"* they were built of rough-hewn local stone and covered in crude plaster. Most had steps leading up to second storey rooms or flat roofs - the favorite place to eat and sleep in the warm Mediterranean climate.

Coarse wool was dyed, spun and woven, usually on an upright loom like this.

Cooking was done on low stoves.

Part of the house was set aside for work. Women would spin and weave, while the men would farm or follow the basic crafts common to the ancient world: as carpenters and builders, tailors, tanners and dyers. A wood-chip behind the ear, a needle in the tunic or a piece of colored cloth would be worn to declare the wearer's trade. No work was done and these symbols would not be worn on the Sabbath.

Roman tools like these were probably standard throughout the Empire.

With wood scarce and most houses built of stone it's no wonder that the original Greek word for Jesus' trade actually means builder, not carpenter.

Life in Jesus' Time

Tools of war

For most of its history the Holy Land was occupied by the armies of conquering Empires. In the time of Jesus it was the military might of Rome that held sway, with nine Roman legions stationed in the east. Together with auxiliaries this meant over 100,000 soldiers. At the height of the First Jewish Revolt Vespasian deployed half these forces against the pitifully armed and untrained Jewish fighters. But the Romans didn't intend doing battle with these upstarts - they came to subdue the countryside and lay siege to the towns.

The Romans used starvation, endless bombardment by catapults and well-protected battering rams to besiege enemy towns.

The basic arms of a legionnaire were his heavy javelin (pila), short thrusting sword and dagger. Protected by helmet, armor and shield - and above all by iron discipline - the Roman army was the greatest fighting force of the ancient world.

JERUSALEM

Its early history

Sacred to the three great monotheistic religions, **Jerusalem** is Yerushalayim - City of Peace - for the Jews, El Quds - the Holy - to Moslems, and Jerusalem for Christians - the city of Christ's crucifixion and resurrection.

At the center of so much faith, Jerusalem has been marched upon by the armies of all the empires of the western world: Egyptians, Philistines, Babylonians, Greeks, Persians, Moslems, Christians, Mameluks, Turks and British, all have laid claim to the city. But for more than three millennia its heart has surrendered to no empire - for Jerusalem is an eternal city, holy to all of human kind.

Buried so deep in the mists of history that only the Bible records the event, an aged nomad once brought his son to a mountain top, ready to sacrifice him to an invisible God. This act of faith - outstanding in a world ruled by pagan idol-worship - caused the young boy to be spared by God,

and his aged father to be granted a covenant that was to last throughout all time. The patriarch, of course, was Abraham, his son, Isaac, and the mountain was **Mount Moriah**.

Centuries later King David captured a fortified hilltop town from the local Canaanite tribe of Jesubites. Changing its name from *"Ursalem"*, David made it his capital and brought the Ark of the Covenant here. This tabernacle, a tent holding the Ten Commandments, was placed on the threshing floor of Ornan on Mount Moriah just outside the city, 2 Samuel 6. One can only wonder if David could have imagined that he was

setting the scene for events that would still be celebrated three thousand years later.

King David was followed by his son Solomon, who is remembered for his legendary wisdom. Solomon was granted the honor of raising a house for the Lord God. The Phoenician king, Hiram of Tyre sent famed Cedars of Lebanon and skilled craftsmen to help built the magnificent Temple, which was adorned with gold and decorated with huge gilded cherubim as described in the second book of Chronicles 3.

And I saw a new heaven and a new earth: for the first heaven and the first earth were passed away;...And I John saw the holy city, new Jerusalem, coming down from God out of heaven

Revelation 21:1-2

JERUSALEM

The Temple and the coming of Christ

Finished in 955 BC, Solomon's Temple stood for four hundred years until the Babylonians invaded Israel. In 587, King Nebuchadnezzar carried the Jews off into Exile and destroyed the Temple. Rebuilt upon their return, the Second Temple was just a shadow of the glory of the first.

A finely worked prayer shawl and ram's horn trumpet - symbols of Jewish roots that pre-date even Solomon's Temple.

Occupied by the Greeks in 333 BC, Alexander the Great allowed the Jews to maintain their religion - but still their Hellenistic culture was hated by many of the Jewish people. When Emperor Antiochus Epiphanes IV proclaimed himself divine, prohibited the practice of Judaism and ordered the sacrifice of pigs in the Temple, the widespread discontent ignited into a full-scale rebellion.

The Maccabean Revolt ousted the Greeks, and in 165 BC they began an independent Hasmonean dynasty that ruled until the coming of Rome in 63 BC. It was then that the great Roman general, Pompey, led his legions into Jerusalem. Fascinated by tales of the great Jewish Temple, he insisted on entering the Inner Sanctum where only Jewish priests were allowed to go.

O Jerusalem, Jerusalem, thou that killest the prophets, and stones them which are sent unto thee … Behold, your house is left unto you desolate.
And Jesus went out, and departed from the temple: and his disciples came to him for to shew him the buildings of the temple. And Jesus said unto them, See ye not all these things? Verily I say unto you, There shall not be left here one stone upon another, that shall not be thrown down.
Matthew 23:37 - 24:2

For generations it was called the Wailing Wall, the last vestige of the second Temple. Renamed the Western Wall, it is now also a source of holy celebration.

This strong-arm disregard for Jewish law was to be the hallmark of the Roman rule.

Jesus foresaw the destruction of the Temple that was to take place in 70 AD at the hands of the Roman general, Titus, who put down the first Jewish rebellion. Titus' plunder of the Temple is vividly recorded on the triumphal Titus Arch in Rome.

A model of the white limestone Temple that stood out above the platform raised to house it. The red arrow marks the Western Wall.

In 132 AD the Jews rebelled again. Led by Simon Bar Kochba - Son of a Star - the Jews won back control of Judea and Samaria, and for two and a half years Jerusalem was again its capital. The Emperor Hadrian sent eight Roman legions and auxiliaries - well over 100,000 men - to put down the rebellion. Determined to finally stamp out all resistance, they destroyed towns and villages and razed Jerusalem to the ground. On its ashes Hadrian erected a Roman colony Aelia Capitolina, and forbade Jews to enter on pain of death. To blot out the name of Judea he renamed

it *Palestina*, and dispersed the Jewish people into exile.

With Jerusalem reduced to rubble, all that was left of the Temple was an outer, retaining wall of the precinct. Known for generations as the Wailing Wall, this became the Jews' holiest place of prayer - the closest they could come to the site of the sacred Temple. Since the re-unification of the city in 1967 it has been renamed **the Western Wall** - and is no longer only a source of sadness.

Many believe that it was to this corner of the Temple that the Devil brought Jesus in the second of the Temptations.

JERUSALEM

Reconstruction to rediscovery

In the fourth century AD, Emperor Constantine embraced the new religion born in the Holy Land. The Roman ruler and his mother, Queen Helena, built churches at all the major sites associated with the life of Christ - especially at Jerusalem's **Holy Sepulchre** - and inspired pilgrimage by converts throughout the Empire.

This flaring of Christianity lasted for three centuries, until the Persian invasion of 614 destroyed many of the shrines. Seventy-four years later the caliph Omar I (or Umar) led the conquering Moslem armies into the Holy Land. This began a 400-year transformation of Jerusalem into Islam's third most sacred city. Recognizing Abraham, David and Solomon as prophets, until today Moslems hold Jerusalem in such esteem that they call it simply El Quds - the Holy.

Christianity returned in force in 1099. Inspired by Pope Urban II, for three years European knights fought their way from Europe into the heart of the Middle East. Storming the walls of Jerusalem just after Moslem prayers on Friday July 15, the Crusaders occupied the city in a frenzy of slaughter. Thus began the liberation of all the Holy sites from the hands of the "infidels".

The Crusaders placed a cross atop the al-Aqsa Mosque, turning it into their Temple, and rebuilt the Holy Sepulchre. With Jerusalem again a city of churches and monasteries, pilgrims came from throughout Christendom. This continued until it was retaken in 1187 by the united Moslem forces under Saladin.

From the end of the 13th century the city became a neglected backwater of the Middle East, and "Jerusalem" in Christian minds turned into more of a romantic ideal than an actual place.

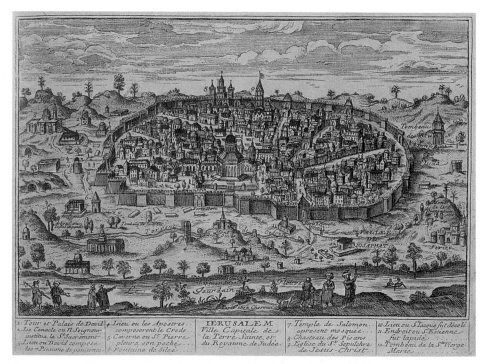

Ancient maps of Jerusalem abound, many placing the city at the center of the world.

This changed with the arrival of a new generation of 19th century European travelers, like British artist David Roberts. His serialized edition of lithographs brought vivid images of the Holy Land to Christian homes, reminding them that Jerusalem was a real city. Published during a new wave of political interest in the Holy Land, his work became a European bestseller. Ironically Roberts himself was more impressed with Jerusalem from outside the walls than from within. His journal reads, *"the city within the walls may be called a desert, two-thirds of it being a mess of ruins and cornfields; the remaining third ... being of such a paltry and contemptible character that no artist could render them interesting"*. Despite the disparaging remark, Roberts' genius did just that.

The Holy Sepulchre from above. The view east takes in the Dome of the Rock with the Mount of Olives beyond.

Roberts' vivid paintings were to have a profound effect on Europe's image of the Holy Land.

JERUSALEM

The modern era

As the Turkish Empire crumbled, Europe's colonial powers vied to win control of the Holy Land. In 1917, General Allenby's forces liberated Jerusalem paving the way for the British mandate. However, decades of Arab-Jewish unrest and growing international pressure after the Nazi Holocaust caused Britain to return the mandate in 1947 and the UN partitioned Palestine.

On May 14, 1948 the State of Israel was declared - and within hours war broke out. After months of desperate fighting the independence of Israel was secured - but Jerusalem was left a divided city. The sound of snipers' bullets echoed across the divide until it was reunited by the Six Day War of 1967 - to the celebration of the Jews and the sorrow of the Palestinians. Now the world watches as efforts are made to finally reach a lasting peace for this eternal city.

Modern excavations paint a picture of ancient magnificence. Clearly visible are the steps that led up from David's City into Herod's Temple precinct on Mount Moriah.

And Hezekiah's Tunnel

Rising in the Kidron Valley, **the Gihon Spring** was Jerusalem's only water source throughout its long history. The second book of Samuel 5, tells how David infiltrated men through the Jesubite's water shaft as he moved to conquer the city.

Centuries later in 701 BC, King Hezekiah faced the approach of the invading Assyrian army as described in the Old Testament books of 2 Kings 18 and 2 Chronicles 32.

The pool of Siloam and the entrance to Hezekiah's Tunnel.

visitors can walk the length of this underground tunnel that stretches from the Gihon Spring to the Pool of Siloam.

In the Gospel of John we read that it was to **the Pool of Siloam** (also called Siloah) that Jesus sent a blind man to wash and regain his sight. The waters of the pool are still believed by many to have therapeutic effects, and people from all religions gather here to be healed.

Running 1,690 feet (512m) underground, Hezekiah's tunnel is a wonder of ancient engineering.

The Kidron Valley, location of the Gihon Spring.

Fearful of the coming siege, he set two gangs of men to excavate an underground tunnel from the spring to within the safety of the walls. Working non-stop day and night, incredibly the two groups met precisely - meters under the earth. Having secured Jerusalem's water supply, **Hezekiah's Tunnel** allowed the city to outlast the Assyrian siege. Till today experts are baffled by this feat of ancient engineering, and

I must work the works of him that sent me, while it is day: the night cometh, when no man can work. As long as I am in the world, I am the light of the world. When he had thus spoken, he spat on the ground, and made caly of the spittle, and he anointed the eyes of the blind man with the clay, and said unto him, Go, wash in the pool of Siloam ... He went his way therefore, and washed, and came seeing.

John 9:4-7

Jesus visited Jerusalem many times before the fateful Passover week. He sometimes taught, sometimes healed. Seeing their authority threatened, the Temple establishment watched His actions with suspicion. One such occasion was the healing Jesus performed at the Pools of Bethesda. They claimed it was unlawful because He had told the lame man to take up his bed and walk, thus breaking the law prohibiting work on the Sabbath. Jesus answered saying, *"My Father*

worketh hitherto, and I work. Therefore the Jews sought the more to kill him, because he not only had broken the sabbath, but said also that God was his Father, making himself equal with God" , John 5:17-18.

Now there is at Jerusalem by the sheep market a pool, which is called in the Hebrew tongue Bethesda, having five porches. ... And a certain man was there, which had an infirmity thirty and eight years. When Jesus saw him lie, and knew that he had been now a long time in that case, he saith unto him, Wilt thou be made whole? The impotent man answered him, Sir, I have no man, when the water is troubled, to put me into the pool: but while I am coming, another steppeth down before me. Jesus saith unto him, Rise, take up thy bed and walk. And immediately the man was made whole, and took up his bed, and walked.

John 5:2-9

The remains of the Pools of Bethesda were discovered by the White Fathers while excavating the grounds of St. Anne's Church. The largest is 350 feet long, 200 wide and 40 deep (105 x 60 x 13m).

Near the five pools a medieval convent was erected in Crusader times.

THE CHURCH OF ST. ANNE

Since as early as the 2nd or 3rd century AD the site of **the Church of St. Anne**, just inside St. Stephen's Gate to the north of the Temple Mount, has been regarded as the birthplace of the Virgin Mary, the home of her parents Anne and Joachim. In the 4th century a basilica to St. Mary was erected here, probably by the Empress Eudoxia.

Toward the end of the 11th century the Crusaders built a small chapel over the fifth century ruins. This they extensively rebuilt in 1140. St. Anne's is recognized by many as the jewel among all the churches the Crusaders built in the city. The building is not symmetrical, suggesting it lies over the foundations of one of the earlier churches, part of which can still be seen in the crypt.

After the Crusaders lost Jerusalem, Saladin turned St. Anne's into a Moslem theological seminary which saved it from destruction. But afterwards, it fell into ruin until the late 19th century when worship there was reinstated.

Detail of a Crusader pillar.

St. Anne's is a jewel of medieval architecture. It shows clearly how the Crusaders built their churches like fortresses.

The Church of the Pater Noster is rooted in the very heart of the New Testament. Although the Gospel of Matthew has Jesus teach the Lord's Prayer in the Galilee, adding to it the immortal words *"for thine is kingdom, and the power, and the glory, for ever. Amen"*, Luke's version places the event somewhere in Jerusalem. Tradition has long seen that as being on the Mount of Olives, and Constantine built a church here named the Eleona - of the olive tree.

The cloister of the Pater Noster is part of the Carmelite convent.

Following the country-wide pattern, this church was destroyed by the Persians and on its ruins the Crusaders erected a new one that they called Pater Noster. It was built over two grottos - one where Jesus *"revealed to his disciples inscrutable mysteries"*, the other called the Grotto of the Pater.

After the expulsion of the Crusaders the area fell into ruin once again until the mid-19th century when the Princess de la Tour

The Grotto of the Pater - said to be where Christ taught the disciples to pray.

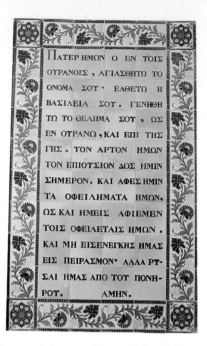

Πατερ ημων ο εν τοις ουρανοις, αγιασθητω το ονομα σου· ελθετω η βασιλεια σου. γενηθη τω το θελημα σου, ως εν ουρανω, και επι της γης. τον αρτον ημων τον επιουσιον δος ημιν σημερον. και αφες ημιν τα οφειληματα ημων, ως και ημεις αφιεμεν τοις οφειλεταις ημων. και μη εισενεγκης ημας εις πειρασμον· αλλα ρυσαι ημας απο του πονηρου. αμην.

Decorated plaques celebrate the Lord's Prayer in sixty-two languages.

And it came to pass, that, as he was praying in a certain place, when he ceased, one of the disciples said unto him, Lord, teach us to pray, as John also taught his disciples. And he said unto them, When ye pray, say, Our Father which art in heaven, Hallowed be thy name. Thy kingdom come. Thy will be done, as in heaven, so in earth. Give us day by day our daily bread. And forgive us our sins; for we also forgive every one that is indebted to us. And lead us not into temptation; but deliver us from evil.

Luke 11:1-4

D'Auvergne arrived from Italy. She purchased the site and lived there in a wooden chalet for eight years, before building a convent which she gave to the Carmelite Sisters. The princess returned to Florence where she died in 1889. Her last wish was to be buried in the cloister. This wish was fulfilled in 1952.

BETHANY

Raising Lazarus from the dead was the greatest miracle Jesus performed in **Bethany**, but of no less significance was His being anointed in the House of Simon the Leper, Mark 14:1-9. The very name Messiah comes from the Hebrew meaning the anointed one, thus it was an important act of confirmation. It also gave Jesus an opportunity to sharply remind the disciples that His earthly days were coming to an end.

These events made Bethany a magnet for the Early Christians, and by the 4th century a church stood over **the Tomb of**

Then said Martha unto Jesus, Lord, if thou hadst been here, my brother had not have died. But I know that even now, whatsoever thou wilt ask of God, God will give it thee. Jesus saith unto her, Thy brother shall rise again. Martha said unto him, I know that he shall rise again in the resurrection of the last day.
Jesus said unto her, I am the resurrection, and the life: he that believeth in me, though he were dead, yet shall he live: And whosoever liveth and believeth in me shall never die.

John 11:21-26

Below the altar's modern fresco, Jesus' words read "I am the resurrection and the life".

Lazarus and later another was erected nearby over the house of Mary and Martha. The remains of these buildings have been incorporated into the structure of the present church, and the tomb is still accessible. A field further up the hill is called **the House of Simon the Leper**. Although no houses were found there, excavations have shown that the area was once occupied, being full of caves, and cisterns.

Inside this ancient doorway twenty-four steps lead down to the Tomb of Lazarus.

The silver domed Church of Lazarus recalls Bethany's most famous event, the raising of Lazarus from the dead.

THE MOUNT OF OLIVES

And in the daytime he was teaching in the Temple; and at night he went out, and abode in the mount that is called the mount of Olives.

Luke 21:37

The daily route Jesus took in and out of the city passed over the **Mount of Olives**. From ancient times the revered rise overlooking Jerusalem from the east was seen with importance.

It was here that Ezekiel 11:23 says, *"the glory of the Lord went up from the midst of the city, and stood upon the mountain which is upon the east side of the city"*, and Zechariah 14:3 prophesied *"Then shall the Lord go forth, and fight against those nations, as when he fought in the day of battle. And his feet shall stand in that day upon the mount of Olives, which is before Jerusalem on the east"*.

One of the cemetery's many ancient tombstones.

It was while crossing these slopes, the day after He cleared the Temple of merchants and moneychangers, that Jesus cursed the fig tree, Matthew 21:18 and Mark 11:13.

The southern slopes of this hill are dominated by the Jerusalem's enormous graveyard - believed to be the oldest continuously used cemetery in the world. Here new graves can be found near those dug over 4,000 years ago. Westward the summit affords great views of the Judean Desert right across to the Mountains of Gilead and Moab.

Generations have chosen burial on the Mount of Olives in order to be as close as possible to the Temple Mount on Judgement Day.

DOMINUS FLEVIT

The memory of Jesus weeping over the fate of Jerusalem has been kept alive for generations, but only since the Crusader times has a church stood here to recall the event. Erected in 1955, the tender quality of **the Church of Dominus Flevit** - the Lord Wept - is augmented by its pleasant garden. This is the last chapel designed by the great Italian architect, Antonio Berluzzi, who died in Rome in 1960 after giving so much to the Holy Land.

Not far from the church is the spot where Jesus delivered what has become known as the Olivet Discourse. This prophetic answer that Jesus gave to the disciples'

Springtime almond blossoms surround the tear-shaped church.

questions regarding the end of days, stretches over two chapters of Matthew's Gospel. It begins, *"And as he sat upon the mount of Olives, the disciples came to him privately, saying, Tell us, when shall these things be? And what shall be the sign of thy coming, and of the end of the world?"*, Matthew 24:3ff.

And when he was come near, he beheld the city, and wept over it, saying, If thou hadst known, even thou, at least in this thy day, the things which belong unto thy peace! but now they are hid from thine eyes.

Luke 19:41-42

Jerusalem's skyline seen through the window of the Berluzzi church.

The Church of Mary Magdalene

In the 19th century Europe "rediscovered" the Holy Land, and the colonial powers began extensively building throughout the country for their pilgrims, especially in Jerusalem. One of Russia's foremost contributions was the **Church of St. Mary Magdalene**, commissioned by Czar Alexander III. It was dedicated to Mary Magdalene, the patroness saint of his family - the ill-fated Romanov dynasty.

John's is the only gospel to name Mary as the woman who anointed Jesus in the house of Simon the Leper (page 115), and whether this was in fact Mary Magdalene or not has been the subject for debate throughout the centuries.

The beautifully decorated interior of the church.

> *Then Mary took a pound of ointment of spikenard, very costly, and anointed the feet of Jesus, and wiped his feet with her hair: and the house was filled with the odor of the ointment.*
>
> John 12:3

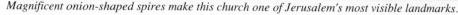

Magnificent onion-shaped spires make this church one of Jerusalem's most visible landmarks.

THE KIDRON VALLEY

Beneath the cemetery on the hillside of the Mount of Olives - and separating it from the Temple Mount - is the barren vale known as **the Kidron Valley**. Legend says that on the Day of Judgement a wire will be stretched over the valley between the two hills, and all who wish to gain entry into the next life will have to walk the wire across the gap.

In the days of the Second Temple Jerusalem's leading families cut grand mausoleums for their dead into the soft rock of the valley floor. The three most recognized are known as **the Pillar of Absalom**, and **the Tombs of St. James** and **Zachariah**.

Although named after the rebellious son of the Biblical king, David, the Pillar of Absalom was in fact built much later, in the first century AD. The tomb of carrying the name of St. James is the entrance to

the catacombs used for generations by one of Jerusalem's most prominent priestly families, the Hezir's. It dates back well over 2,100 years. The Tomb of Zachariah, with its unusual pyramid-shaped roof, is recognized as one of the finest examples of Second Temple period funerary architecture.

The Kidron Valley Tombs are cut into the soft rock at the base of the Mount of Olives.

The Tomb of Zachariah

The Pillar of Absalom

The Tomb of St. James

and 38 tell that when King David was dying, he commanded his son Solomon to be brought on the king's own mule to Gihon to be anointed.

It was almost Pesach, the feast of the Passover, when Jesus came to Jerusalem (John 12). Celebrating the Exodus from Egypt, this week-long festival always brought trouble to the Roman occupied capital. Fueled by the Jews' age-old struggle for spiritual and political freedom, turmoil was the backdrop for the end of Jesus' earthly ministry.

Staying in Bethany, Jesus walked to Jerusalem everyday through **Bethpage** on the slopes of the Mount of Olives. Approaching the village on Sunday, Jesus sent two disciples to obtain a donkey for Him to ride into the city. Thus Matthew 21:1-12 describes how Jesus fulfilled the Old Testament prophecy, *"Behold, thy King comes unto thee, meek, and sitting upon an ass"* . The idea of riding an ass not only marked Jesus' humility but also pointed to His kingly position. 1 Kings 1:33

The Greek church commands a magnificent view from the slopes of the Mount of Olives.

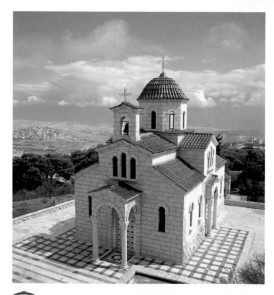

The Franciscan chapel containing the Mounting Stone is in the foreground (left) while a Greek church stands nearer the summit.

When the multitudes called *"Hosanna"* and cut palm fronds, they too were enacting old Jewish customs. Derived from the Hebrew meaning please save, *"Hosanna"* is the cry of the Feast of the Tabernacles when people carry branches of palm, myrtle and willow. It recalls the 40 years after the Exodus, when the Children of Israel wandered in the desert before their triumphant entry into the Promised Land. Not restricted to the festival, such processions also broke out spontaneously, and had already led to several bloody massacres. The Romans were worried about a repeat.

Since as early as the 12th century an annual Holy Week procession has started at Bethpage on the Mount of Olives. Today a Franciscan chapel established in 1883 on the slopes marks its starting place. It contains the **Mounting Stone of Christ** mentioned by the earliest pilgrims as being the stone Christ used when mounting the donkey. The chapel also contains a cubical stone decorated with paintings dating from Cusader times. These show the resurrection of Lazarus, an ass and its foal, people carrying palms, a castle, and a Latin inscription of the name Bethpage.

From here the annual Palm Sunday procession makes its way into the city through the Lions' Gate - also called the Gate of St. Stephen.

For centuries the Palm Sunday procession has made its way down the Mount of Olives and past the Temple Mount.

Much people that were come to the feast, when they heard that Jesus was coming to Jerusalem, took branches of palm trees, and went forth to meet him, and cried Hosanna: Blessed is the King of Israel that cometh in the name of the Lord.

John 12:12-13

Pilgrims enter the city's narrow lanes through the Gate of St. Stephen.

Many myths surround the walls and **the eight gates of Jerusalem's Old City** - one tells of the Ottoman caliph, Suleiman the Magnificent. One night in a dream the four lions that had guarded the throne of Kings David and Solomon came to savage him, as punishment for the heavy taxes he'd imposed upon the city. Waking in a sweat, he cancelled the tax and ordered a two-and-

a-half mile limestone wall to be built around Jerusalem instead. Where the work began in 1538, Suleiman erected a gate adorned with four lions, in memory of his dream.

This is the legend of **the Lions' Gate**, although another version sometimes ascribes it to Sultan Baybars, the 13th century founder of the Mameluk State. The Gate is also called St. Stephen's after the first Christian martyr who was stoned to death here, Acts 7.

The Zion Gate. The walls are constructed on the foundations laid by Herod the Great.

The Lions' Gate is also called St. Stephen's after the first Christian martyr.

Herod's (or Flower) Gate. The house of Herod Antipas was once thought to stand nearby.

The Zion Gate is the entrance to the Jewish Quarter. It is called Bab el Daoud, in Arabic - David's Gate - after the king whose tomb is on Mount Zion opposite.

Taking its name from the garbage that Christians used to throw on the ruins of the Temple in Byzantine times, **the Dung Gate** leads to the Western Wall. Near Herod's Gate, Crusader siege towers breached the walls of the city in 1099. It is the entrance to the Moslem quarter.

The most ornate example of Ottoman design is **the Damascus Gate**, built where the Roman Emperor Hadrian opened a northern entrance nearly 2,000 years ago. Still visible today, his Triple Gate once led onto the city's main thoroughfare.

Roberts captured the timeless quality of the Damascus Gate as the main commercial entrance to the city.

A Moslem tradition says that a destroying conqueror will one day enter the city through **the Golden Gate** - thus the gate is blocked and is guarded by a cemetery. The Jews believe that the Messiah will enter Jerusalem from here. For Christians it marks the place where Jesus Christ indeed entered the Temple Mount. Standing above the Susa Gate, the entrance to the area called Solomon's Porch in Acts 3:11, it is where early Christians gathered to meet.

A night view of the New Gate, opened in 1889.

> *I was glad when they said unto me, Let us go into the house of the Lord. Our feet shall stand in thy gates, Oh Jerusalem.*
>
> Psalm 122

The only gap in Suleiman's wall is one facing west, where **the Jaffa Gate** was widened in 1889 for Germany's Kaiser Wilhelm II to enter the city in his carriage. At the same time **the New Gate** was opened to give access to the Christian Quarter.

The Golden Gate, also called the Gate of Mercy.

The Jaffa Gate.

With rich aromas, rainbow colors and exotic flavors spices from around the globe are a feast for the senses.

Above the rooftops of **Jerusalem's Old City** chiming church bells, the chants of *muezzins* calling to the Moslem faithful, and the murmur of Jewish prayer all blend together. Following a tradition established in the Middle Ages, the Old City is divided into four quarters - Christian, Jewish, Moslem and Armenian. Each boasts its own sights and sounds, but all preserve the time-honored tradition of the market trade characteristic of the Levant. The *shuk* is filled with the pungent aromas of spices and the resonant cries of street vendors.

Running down from the Jaffa Gate, Omar ibn el-Khattab Street is a kaleidoscope of ever-changing color.

The Old City's bazaars are renowned for their leather- and wood-work, and their traditional embroidered clothing.

Traditional drink vendors serve chilled date juice by the Damascus Gate.

Jerusalem's markets are a tapestry of varied colors. Goods from all over the world find their way into the Old City's narrow, winding alleys, on carts stills driven by human muscle power alone. But don't stand in the way of one of these - their only braking system is an old rubber tire chained to the back that is jumped on by the "driver".

The unique decoration characteristic of the Armenian ceramic artisans.

MOUNT ZION

The Church of the Dormition

Mount Zion is hallowed for the Last Supper, the Apparition of the Risen Christ and the Descent of the Holy Spirit, all of which are said to have occurred here. It is also where long held tradition says the Virgin Mary lived after the death of her Son, and where she finally fell into her eternal sleep. Today's **Church of the Dormition** maintains this tradition, with a wall mosaic depicting the Madonna and Child in the apse and a cherry-wood and ivory statue of the sleeping Mary in the crypt. This magnificent modern edifice was erected in 1906 upon foundations well rooted in the past.

The title of Mount Zion originally meant only that area occupied by the city built by King David, but later tradition transferred

The interior design of the church was based on Charlemagne's chapel at Aix-la Chapelle. It is decorated with a mosaic of Mary and the child Jesus.

the name to mean the ridge that overlooks the southwest corner of the Old City. This hill was incorporated into the city during Hezekiah's expansion in the 8th century BC, and like the rest of the ancient metropolis, Mount Zion was enclosed within the city walls during the New Testament period.

When Rome's destruction of the city left one church standing on Mount Zion, early Christians heard the words of the Prophet

Isaiah speak directly to them, *"Out of Zion shall go forth the law, and the word of the Lord from Jerusalem"*. Within a few centuries the small chapel had been transformed into the great basilica of Hagia Zion - Holy Zion, that became known as "the Mother of all Churches".

The Crusaders rebuilt upon its ruins, naming their church St. Mary (or Our Mother) of Mount Zion, and included

Great is the Lord, and greatly to be praised in the city of our God, in the mountain of his holiness. Beautiful for situation, the joy of the whole world, is mount Zion, on the sides of the north, the city of the great King.

Psalm 48 -
The Beauty and Glory of Zion

Mount Zion sprinkled with a Jerusalem mid-winter snow.

within it several chapels dedicated to these events, and one to the martyred St. Stephen.

It is told that when Suleiman the Magnificent rebuilt the walls as we know them in the 16th century, his two top city planners somehow forgot to include Mount Zion within the ramparts. Paying dearly for their mistake, the two unfortunate architects were executed.

The Church and Abbey of the Dormition appear like some medieval fortress.

THE CENACLE

And David's Tomb

It was the eve of the Jewish Feast of the Passover, or Unleavened Bread, and Jesus and the disciples retired to an upper room to partake of the traditional Passover celebration. During this meal Jesus washed the feet of the disciples and foretold the coming betrayal. But perhaps of most significance, this was the occasion for Jesus to transform the traditional blessings over bread and wine into the foundation of the Eucharist - a momentous event marked by all four Gospels.

The site of **the Cenacle** on Mount Zion soon became a meeting place for the first Christians. Early pilgrims reported all manner of things connected to the life of Jesus that were kept in the great Basilica of Hagia Zion erected over the original chapel: the horn used for anointing the Kings David and Solomon, the column of the Flagellation, the Crown of Thorns and the Lance that pierced Christ's side.

The Cenacle was built by the Crusaders in memory of the Last Supper.

The structure now carrying the name of the Room of the Last Supper was built by the Franciscans in the 14th century. With firm columns and delicately pointed Gothic arches it was erected over earlier Byzantine and Crusader buildings. A flight of 30 steps leads up to where it formed an "upper room" in the southern wing of the Church of St. Mary of Zion. It was decorated with mosaics depicting both the Eucharist and the Descent of the Holy Ghost. The chapel below it recalled the washing of the feet and the Apparition of the Risen Jesus. To the east was the tomb of St. Stephen.

David's Tomb may originally have been the Tomb of St. Stephen.

The Tomb of David

"So David slept with his fathers, and was buried in the city of David", 1 Kings 2:10. This may either mean Jerusalem's City of David, or refer to Bethlehem. Early Christian pilgrims mention the Tomb of David at the tomb of St. Stephen on Mount Zion, but the first Jewish record comes from a 12th century traveler, Joseph of Tudela. He recalls being told that 15 years earlier a collapsed wall

Detail of a column incorporated into a later Moslem mosque.

And as they did eat, Jesus took bread, and blessed and brake it, and gave to them and said, Take, eat, this is my body. And he took the cup, and when he had given thanks, he gave it to them: and they all drank of it. And he said unto them, This is my blood of the new testament, which is shed for many. Verily I say unto you, I will drink no more of the fruit of the vine, until that day that I drink it new in the kingdom of God. And when they had sung an hymn, they went out into the mount of Olives.

Mark 14:22-26

revealed rich tombs believed to be those of David and Solomon. The tomb's burial stone is covered with a cloth of royal purple - embroidered with David's symbols, the Star and harps. Upon it are crowns that once adorned Torah scrolls, saved from Nazi hands.

THE GARDEN OF GETHSAMANE

And the Church of the Agony

After the Last Supper Jesus walked with the disciples to **the Garden of Gethsemane**, to begin the final steps to the destiny that awaited Him. The Gospel of John 8:1 says that they went *"over the brook Cedron, where there was a garden"*, refering to the Kidron Valley (page 119). The name Gethsemane means oil press, and there seems no reason to doubt the tradition that this is the garden named in Matthew's Gospel. Till today the lower slopes of the Mount of Olives are covered with ancient olive trees, some of which are reckoned to be old enough to have heard Jesus' final words of prayer, *"nevertheless, not my will, but thy will, be done"*, Luke 22:42. Three times Jesus prayed for *"this cup (to) pass from me"*, but it was not to be. After His Agony, Temple guards appeared, led by Judas Iscariot who approached to kiss Him. Luke's Gospel continues that Jesus said, *"Judas, betrayest thou the Son of man with a kiss?"*. Then the Roman soldiers seized Jesus while the disciples fled.

Legend tells that when Christ was finally crucified the trees of all the world shed their leaves - except the Olives. When its brothers and sisters came to ask why, the olive said, *"Yes, you all shed your leaves in sadness, but next spring they will grow anew. I was pierced to the heart, and there is in me now a sorrow that will never heal"*. And so it is that the olive tree does indeed die from the inside outward.

The Church of the Agony

The original 4th century sanctuary was enlarged some 800 years later by the Crusaders and renamed St. Saviors. The present Church of the Agony, completed in 1924, is one of Jerusalem's most beautiful. The Four Evangelists stand atop columns by its arched portico. Over their heads a magnificent mosaic depicts Jesus offering his suffering to God above, who sits holding Greek letters. This captures the

The "parents" of this ancient olive tree may have witnessed the events of that fateful night.

*The Stone of Agony is surrounded by
a wrought iron Crown of Thorns.*

*Built with worldwide contributions this basilica is
also called the Church of All Nations.*

words of Revelation 1:8 *"I am the Alpha
and the Omega, the beginning and the
ending, saith the Lord"*.

Inside, dim light is reflected on dark
blue cupolas dotted with stars representing
the night sky. The Stone of the Agony
dominates the floor of the church, while
its walls are adorned with scenes of that
fateful night.

*Then cometh Jesus with them
unto a place called Gethsemane,
and saith unto the disciples, Sit
ye here, while I go and pray
yonder. And he took with him
Peter and the sons of Zebedee,
and began to be sorrowful and
very heavy.   And he went a little
further, and fell on his face, and
prayed, saying, O my Father, if
it be possible, let this cup pass
from me.*

Matthew 26:36-39

THE TOMB OF MARY

As the soldiers led Jesus away from the Garden of Gethsemane, they would have passed the nearby spot that become **the Tomb of the Virgin Mary**. Though she probably lived and died on Mount Zion tradition holds that she was buried here at the foot of the Mount of Olives. This has led many scholars to conclude that the land around Gethsemane was owned by one of the disciples.

A simple shrine, Mary's Tomb also holds the ashes of the Crusader queen, Millicent.

We are told that being sinless and not subject to the corruption of the flesh Mary was taken directly into heaven. Thus, ever since the first shrine was erected over her tomb in the 5th century, it has also been known as **the Church of the Assumption**.

Three large holes allow visitors to touch the inside of the Tomb of the Virgin.

The Crusaders rebuilt the church as we have it now, and in it laid the ashes of the crusader queen, Millicent. Around it they raised a monastery called the Abbey of St. Mary of the Valley of Jehoshaphat. The Moslems destroyed that monastery and its upper church when they retook Jerusalem, but the Sanctuary itself was spared because they too venerate the Mother of Jesus.

Forty-five steps lead down past chapels of Mary's parents, Anne and Joachim, and her husband Joseph.

ST. PETER IN GALLICANTU

Brought to the House of the High Priest, Caiaphas, Jesus stood before members of the Jewish high court. Here Mark 14:61-62 records, *"Again the high priest asked him, ... Art thou the Christ, the Son of the Blessed? And Jesus said, I am: and ye shall see the Son of man sitting on the right hand of the power, and coming in clouds of heaven"*. It was enough for them to cry blasphemy and imprison Him overnight. As this occurred Peter was identified, but three times he denied being one of Jesus' followers.

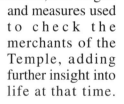

This underground cavern is believed to be where Jesus was imprisoned.

The present church of **St. Peter in Gallicantu** (cock-crow) was raised in an area full of remains of early Jerusalem. Some hold it to be the site of the earliest church by this

Ancient steps lead from Mount Zion towards Gethsemane.

name that stood over the palace of Caiaphas. However, as the Franciscan scholar, F. E. Hoade points out, *"this thesis has not yet gained the vote of archaeologists"*. Many

of them see this as the site of a Byzantine church raised over the grotto where Peter wept in grief, called from the 12th century St. Peter in Gallicantu.

In either case the modern building recalls Peter's denial in mosaics on both the inside and outside of the church - and excavations carried out beneath uncovered a series of chambers, and weights and measures used to check the merchants of the Temple, adding further insight into life at that time.

Close to the Zion Gate is **the Armenian Church of Caiaphas**. Here, archaeologists found dwellings from the Second Temple period, and remains of a Byzantine church and Crusader chapel, next to where the Armenian patriarchs are buried.

The 5th century Byzantines built the first church recalling Peter's triple denial.

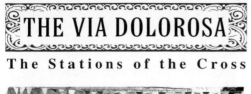

THE VIA DOLOROSA

The Stations of the Cross

The Via Dolorosa starts where the Fortress of Antonia once stood.

The Via Dolorosa, or Way of Sorrow, is the traditional path Jesus took on the fateful journey to the Crucifixion at Calvary. Formalized only in the 16th century, it is nonetheless a route followed since the earliest times of Christianity. The route winds its way from the site of the ancient Fortress of Antonia - in the courtyard of the present El Omarieh college, where Jesus was tried and condemned by Pontius Pilate - to the Church of the Holy Sepulchre.

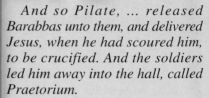

And so Pilate, ... released Barabbas unto them, and delivered Jesus, when he had scoured him, to be crucified. And the soldiers led him away into the hall, called Praetorium.

Mark 15:15-16

I **Jesus is Condemned.**
The First of the Fourteen Stations of the Cross is to be found at the *praetorium* or court of law within the precinct of the Antonia Fortress, where Jesus was brought to trial before Pontius Pilate. On one side of a beautiful Crusader courtyard nearby stands the Church of the Condemnation. It bears a unique painted sculpture that brings alive the scene of Pilate washing his hands of the guilt for Jesus' death.

The Via Dolorosa with the Chapels of the Condemnation and Flagellation on the right.

The Church of the Condemnation depicts Pilate washing his hands of the responsibility for Christ's death.

The Chapel of the Flagellation shows the bound Saviour beneath the crown of thorns.

 Jesus takes up the Cross.

Built on the ruins of a Crusader oratory across the same courtyard is the modest **Chapel of the Flagellation**. Its stained glass windows show Jesus bound and scoured. On the ceiling is a crown of thorns, in memory of the event told of in the Gospels *"And they clothed him with purple, and platted a crown of thorns, and put it about his head, and began to salute him, Hail, King of the Jews"*, Mark 15:17-18. Outside the chapel is the pavement where Jesus took up the cross he was to be crucified upon as a common criminal.

Every Friday a procession sets out to retrace the Stations of the Cross.

This image celebrates Jesus taking up the cross.

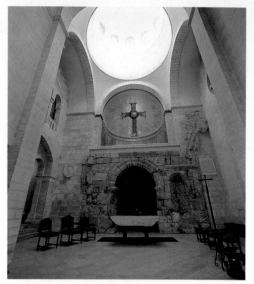

When the Via Dolorosa was established, **the Ecce Homo Arch** was thought to be the doorway of the Antonia Fortress through which Pilate brought Jesus before the crowds with the words, "Behold the Man" - Ecce Homo in Latin. Now it is known to have been part of the triumphant triple-arched entrance to Emperor Hadrian's Aelia Capitolina, raised in 135 AD. Part of the remaining arch is visible inside the Convent

Then came Jesus forth, wearing the crown of thorns, and the purple robe. And Pilate saith unto them, Behold the man!

John 19:5

The Chapel of Ecce Homo inside the convent of the Sisters of Zion.

of the Sisters of Zion, where the Lithostrotos pavement can also be seen.

The Lithostrotos is a section of the original Roman pavement from the Antonia Fortress. Made up of large stone slabs, one of them is etched for a game of chance called the King's Game. The Roman soldiers used this for gambling, or for dividing up the clothes of those condemned to die, *"they parted his garments, casting lots upon them"*, Mark 15:24.

The balcony of the convent offers great views over Jerusalem's rooftops.

A model of the Antonia Fortress that overlooked the Temple - home to the Roman garrison.

Originally built by Herod the Great as a palace, **the Antonia Fortress** was named after his Roman friend and mentor, Marc Anthony. By the time Pontius Pilate became prefect of Judea in 26 AD, its four huge, imposing towers had become a symbol of the Roman domination of Jerusalem, and the main barracks of its forces in the city. It is believed that here Pilate tried Jesus.

Beneath the pavement are the ancient double cisterns known as the Struthion Pools (page 39).

When Pilate therefore heard that saying, he brought Jesus forth, and sat down in the judgement seat in a place that is called the Pavement.

John 19:13

The original stone pavement was roughened so people and beasts of burden would not slip.

The arch of Ecce Homo spans the Via Dolorosa.

Roman soldiers played on a board cut into the pavement.

III **Jesus falls for the first time**. Sculptures both above the door and inside the Polish chapel, recall Jesus' first fall. Outside the church built by Polish servicemen brought to Jerusalem by World War II, pilgrims often stop and read the words of Lamentations 1:16 *"the comforter that should relieve my soul is far from me"*.

IV **Jesus meets His Mother**. Several of the stations recall events not mentioned in the Gospels themselves but maintained by tradition. The Fourth Station, by the Church of Our Lady of the Spasm, is one of those. Its spirit was captured by the Franciscan poet, Fra Jacopone, *"Who could mark, from*

tears refraining, Christ's dear Mother uncomplaining, In so great a sorrow bowed".

Inside the church a Byzantine mosaic depicts two feet pointing northwest. These are believed to be where Mary stood as she gazed upon the sufferings of her Son.

IV Jesus meets His mother.

III Jesus falls for the first time.

V Simon of Cyrene helps Jesus carry the cross.

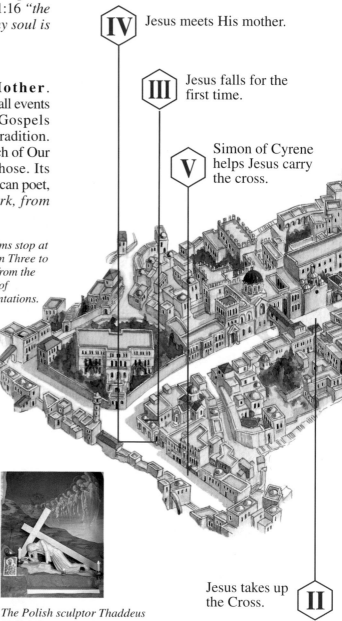

Pilgrims stop at Station Three to read from the Book of Lamentations.

Station Four is where Jesus saw His Mother.

The Polish sculptor Thaddeus Zieliensky captured the moment Jesus fell for the first time beneath the weight of the cross.

II Jesus takes up the Cross.

*Station Five is where
Simon the Cyrene took
the cross from Jesus.*

V

**Simon of
Cyrene helps Jesus
carry the cross**. Simon, the man of
Cyrene in North
Africa was
compelled to carry
the cross for Jesus.
He is unmentioned
elsewhere in the Gospels, but
his children, Alexander and
Rufus - mentioned by Mark - are known
from other sources as members of Jerusalem's
early Christian community.

I   Jesus is Condemned.

VI   **Veronica wipes the face of Jesus.**
About eighty paces bring one to the Armenian
Church where a fragment of an ancient column
in the wall marks the Sixth Station of the Cross. Here,
Veronica wiped the brow of Jesus leaving an impression
of His face on her veil. This has been kept in St. Peter's
in Rome since 707.

Tradition has it that this lady, who showed both courage
and charity, is the same as the one described in Matthew
9:21 who was healed by touching Jesus' garment.

*The doorway to the Armenian
church where Veronica is recalled.*

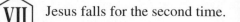

VII	Jesus falls for the second time.
VIII	Jesus consoles the daughters of Jerusalem.
IX	Jesus falls for the third time.
X	Jesus is stripped of His garments.
XI	Jesus is nailed to the Cross.
XII	Jesus dies on the Cross.
XIII	Jesus is taken down from the Cross.
XIV	Jesus is laid in the tomb.

No words can describe the suffering felt that day - or this.

 ## Jesus falls for the second time.

The road rises towards Station Seven where a Roman column stands to the right of the altar, near the spot where tradition places Jesus' second fall. It is said that a Gate of Judgement stood here, through which Jesus passed on His way out of the city. On the gate the authorities would post notices announcing the sentences passed on convicted criminals.

And there followed him a great company of people, and of women which also bewailed and lamented him. But Jesus turning unto them said, Daughters of Jerusalem, weep not for me but weep for yourselves, and for your children.

Luke 23:27-28

VIII Jesus consoles the daughters of Jerusalem.

A Latin cross marks the eighth station of the Via Dolorosa. Carved into the stone wall by the cross is the Greek word NIKA - meaning Victor. Here, knowing the future devastation that awaits them, Jesus consoled the women of Jerusalem.

A small Latin cross carved into the stone wall marks Station Eight.

IX Jesus falls for the third time.

Beside the door of the Coptic Patriarchate is a column marking where Jesus fell for the third and last time as He approached the summit of Calvary. Left of the doorway is a courtyard that was once the refectory

The column with a cross, left of the doorway, marks the 9th Station of the Cross.

VI

Veronica wipes the face of Jesus.

of the Crusader Canons of the Holy Sepulchre. Its remains are clearly visible in the walls, arches and columns that once held a magnificent vaulted ceiling but now stand open to the sky.

Today the courtyard forms the backdrop for tiny, brightly painted hermitages that house a community of Ethiopian monks. It is also the roof of the underground **Chapel of St. Helena** whose cupola emerges at its center. This covers **the Crypt of the Invention - or the Finding - of the Cross**, where Queen Helena is said to have found some of the wood of the Cross. Rebuilt in 11th century and supported by four beautiful Crusader pillars, Helena's chapel is reached down stairs leading from within the main body of the church. The stone walls by the stairs are covered with hundreds of carved crosses - ancient graffiti left by Crusader soldiers.

Crusader crosses, medieval graffiti left on the walls leading down to the Chapel of St. Helena.

For centuries the heart of Christian Jerusalem has been **the Church of the Holy Sepulchre**. Erected in memory of the final events of Christ's Passion - where Jesus was crucified, buried and rose again - this magnificent basilica is a fitting home to the last five Stations of the Cross.

Associated with legends of Adam's tomb, a small rise just outside the city walls had long reminded Jerusalem residents of a human skull, Golgotha in Aramaic. An ancient quarry here had been turned into the city's burial ground, with family tombs cut into the rock (Beth Shearim necropolis, pages 80/1). Under Roman occupation the "place of the skull" became where they crucified common criminals - and Jesus Christ.

For over a century the early Christians preserved the memory of Christ's crucifixion and resurrection here despite increasing Roman persecution. Emperor Hadrian finally destroyed Jerusalem in 135 AD and covered the site with a shrine to Venus and a statue of Jupiter. When Constantine adopted Christianity two centuries later, his mother Helena came on a pilgrimage and found that Hadrian had not razed Christ's tomb as feared, only covered it with rubble. Clearing this away work was completed on the first great basilica here in 335.

A golden cross tops the Rotunda above the Tomb of Christ.

Burned by the Persians in the 7th century, Constantine's original basilica was rebuilt only to be destroyed again in 1009 by the Arab caliph al-Hakim. Restored a generation later, it was the sorry state of Christianity's core symbol that ignited Europe to the passion of the Holy Crusades.

Entering Jerusalem in 1099 and finding the new structure unsuitable, the Crusaders rebuilt the church, extending it to include the site of the crucifixion at Calvary not part of Constantine's original monument. Since then the Church of the Holy Sepulchre has suffered fire, earthquake, wars and natural deterioration. The last major construction was carried out in the 19th century, giving the final touches to a church that is now visited by millions every year.

This painting shows the Church of the Holy Sepulchre as it was 140 years ago.

And he bearing his cross went forth into a place called the place of a skull, which is called in the Hebrew Golgotha; where they crucified him.

John 19:17-18

Built in 326 AD, the Church of the Holy Sepulchre is the focus of Christian pilgrimage.

THE HOLY SEPULCHRE

Stations 10-12

Inside the entrance to the Church of the Holy Sepulchre a narrow flight of steps ascends 15 feet (4.5m) up what tradition says was the final slope to the summit of Calvary - to the place of the crucifixion itself.

> *And they crucified him, and parted his garments, casting lots.*
>
> Matthew 27:35

X **Jesus is stripped of His garments.** At the top of the stairs is **the Chapel of the Divestiture**. This marks where Roman soldiers stripped Jesus in preparation for His crucifixion, and divided His clothes among them.

> *Now there stood by the cross of Jesus his mother, and his mother's sister, Mary the wife of Cleophas, and Mary Magdalene.*
>
> John 19:25

XI **Jesus is nailed to the Cross.** Of the many rich mosaics that covered the walls and ceiling of Calvary in Crusader times only one portrait of Jesus remains. The other mosaics now seen were all executed in the middle of the last century. The mosaic above the altar shows Jesus being nailed to the cross, watched by the Holy women.

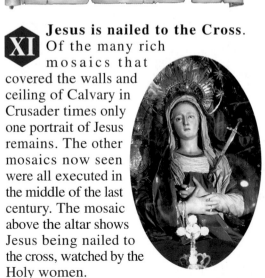

Mary the Mother of Christ is seen pierced to the heart.

A mosaic shows Jesus being nailed to the Cross.

To the left of this mosaic is a small altar dedicated to the heartbreak of Mary. Named **the Mater Dolorosa**, Our Lady of Suffering, it recalls the prophecy Simeon made when Mary and Joseph brought the infant Jesus to the Temple, *"Yea, a sword shall pierce through thy own heart also"*, Luke 2:35. Crafted in the 1500's, this beautiful painted wooden statue was presented to the church by Maria I of Portugal in 1778.

> *He said unto Jesus, Lord, remember me when thou comest into thy kingdom. And Jesus said unto him, Verily I say unto thee, Today shalt thou be with me in paradise.*
>
> Luke 23:42-43

XII **Jesus dies on the Cross.** All Four Gospels tell how Christ was crucified by the Romans next to two common criminals beneath a sign reading *"This is Jesus the King of the Jews"*. The spot where Jesus' cross stood is marked by a silver disc beneath the altar, while black marble discs to either side mark those of the criminals.

Matthew chapter 27 describes the moment of Jesus' death, *"Jesus, when he had cried out again in a loud voice, yielded up the ghost. And, behold, the veil of the temple was rent in twain from the top to the bottom; and the earth did quake and the rocks rent"*. Then the Centurion watching over Him declared, *"Truly this was the Son of God"*.

To thc right of thc altar is seen the original bedrock of Calvary showing the rent caused by that earthquake - a split in the rock that runs down into **the Chapel of Adam** below. Tradition says that thus the blood of Christ spilled down upon the head of the first sinner of mankind. That is why Adam's skull is often represented at the foot of the Cross.

Also recalled at the Twelfth Station are Jesus' words from Luke's Gospel 23:46, *"he said, Father, into thy hands I commend my spirit; and having said thus, he gave up the ghost"*.

Jesus Dies on the Cross - with icons of the Virgin Mother and the disciple John beside Him.

THE HOLY SEPULCHRE

Station 13

After Jesus died on the Cross, His companions - the disciples and close family - still had several hours of agony before they could receive the body. They witnessed soldiers breaking the legs of the two criminals next to Jesus to prevent them remaining alive on the cross during the Passover Sabbath. But finding Jesus already dead, one soldier simply thrust a spear into His side.

This was the beginning of a legend concerning the spear of the legionnaire Longinus. That spear is said to have been found by the Crusaders just outside Antioch in June 1098, and helped lead them into victorious battles. The soldier himself is remembered in **the Chapel of St. Longinus** situated along the gallery formed by seven 11th century arches, known as **the Arches of the Virgin**.

But when they came to Jesus and saw that he was dead already, they brake not his legs: But one of the soldiers with a spear pierced his side.

John 19:33-34

XIII **Jesus is taken down from the Cross.**

The Stone of the Unction, the thirteenth, Station of the Cross is the first thing one meets upon entering the Church of the Holy Sepulchre. It is situated at the foot of Calvary and although the Gospels describe Mary watching events from nearby, tradition depicts her receiving the body of Jesus into her arms as it was slowly lowered from the Cross by Joseph of Arimethaea - a disciple and member of the Jewish counsel. It was onto this Unction, or Anointing Stone that the body of Christ was laid to be prepared for burial.

And Joseph of Arimathaea, being a disciple of Jesus, ... besought Pilate that he might take away the body of Jesus: and Pilate gave him leave. ... And there came also Nicodemus ... and brought a mixture of myrrh and aloes, about an hundred pound weight. Then they took the body of Jesus and wound it in linen clothes with the spices.

John 19:38-40

A mosaic above the Unction Stone depicts Jesus being taken down from the Cross, prepared for burial, and placed in the Tomb.

Beneath the balcony that marks Calvary, the Stone of the Unction (Anointing) is where Jesus was laid when brought down from the Cross.

THE HOLY SEPULCHRE

Station 14 - Jesus' Tomb

XIV **Jesus is laid in the tomb.**
It was already coming on towards evening when Jesus' lifeless body was brought down from the Cross, with little time left before the Passover Sabbath. The newly cut tomb of Joseph of Arimathea stood ready nearby, and to this double-roomed cave - the Holy Sepulchre itself - Jesus was carried and laid in the innermost chamber, either on a ledge or in a stone coffin as was the custom of the time.

A great round stone was then rolled over the entrance to seal the tomb.

Today, Joseph of Arimethea's subterranean tomb is the Tomb of Jesus, an ornate structure built over the original two chambers. The outer chamber, called **the Chapel of the Angel**, is larger and would have been where the family gathered to mourn. It is marvelously decorated with fine carvings in white marble. The doorway to the

And when Joseph had taken the body, he wrapped it in a clean linen cloth, and laid it in his own new tomb, which he had hewn out in the rock: and he rolled a great stone to the door of the sepulchre, and departed.

Matthew 27:59-60

The outer chamber of the tomb is called the Chapel of the Angel.

The tombstone of Jesus - the Holiest place in the Christian world.

inner chamber illustrates the Risen Christ appearing from the coffin (above), the coming of the women on the Sunday with urns of ointment (left), and the angel who proclaimed the resurrection (right).

The smaller mortuary chamber is the heart of the Holy Sepulchre itself. It is here that the body of Jesus rested from that Friday evening until Sunday at sunrise. It is now covered by a smooth white marble slab that was placed there in 1555. Above the tomb are painted scenes depicting Christ's victory over death.

THE HOLY SEPULCHRE

The Anastasis

It was Queen Helena, mother of the Roman Emperor Constantine, who commissioned Bishop Macarius to build the first basilica over the ruins of the ancient tomb of Jesus. They named the circular part of their grandiose church **the Anastasis**, or **Resurrection**. Following the long established pattern of Roman royal mausoleums, all of the surrounding rock was removed leaving only that part of the stone into which the original tomb had been dug. Then - as now - this stood at the center of the Anastasis as **the Tomb of the Redeemer**.

Over the many intervening centuries the structure around the tomb has changed, but the inside of the first chamber still celebrates the event that took place there three days after Jesus was buried. This is called **the Chapel of the Angel** and it is named after the angel (or two angels according to Luke's Gospel) who sat here and announced Christ's Resurrection to the women.

Now upon the first day of the week, very early in the morning, they came unto the sepulchre, bringing the spices which they had prepared, and certain others with them. And they found the stone rolled away from the sepulchre. And they entered in and they found not the body of the Lord Jesus. And it came to pass as they were much perplexed thereabout, behold, two men stood by them in shining garments: and ... they said unto them, Why seek ye the living among the dead? He is not here, but is risen.

Luke 24:1-6

The Holy Sepulchre, the Tomb of Christ, dominates the Rotunda of the church.

The renovated Rotunda above the Tomb of Jesus was unveiled to the public on January 2, 1997.

THE HOLY SEPULCHRE

The Resurrection

Originally part of the 12th century Crusader structure, **the Catholicon** makes up the main body of the basilica opposite the Tomb of Jesus. Containing **the Iconostasis**, a lavishly decorated partition that separates the altar from the congregation, the whole area stands beneath a dome that marks what many Christians believe to be the center of the world.

Slightly to the northeast of the Rotunda is **the Altar of Mary Magdalene**. Said to mark the garden originally surrounding the tomb, it was here the risen Christ appeared for the first time, to Mary Magdelene as she stood weeping.

Next to this altar is **the Church of the Apparition of Jesus to his Mother**. Unmentioned by the Gospels a time-honored tradition holds that Jesus also

Jesus saith unto her, Woman why weepest thou? Whom seekest thou? She, supposing him to be the gardener, saith unto him, Sir, if thou have borne him hence, tell me where thou hast laid him, and I will take him away. Jesus saith unto her, Mary. She turned herself, and saith unto him, Rabboni; which is to say, Master. Jesus saith unto her, Touch me not; for I am not yet ascended to my Father: but go to my brethren and say unto them, I ascend to my Father, and to your Father.

John 20:15-17

appeared to His mother, Mary - and a pleasant Franciscan church preserves the memory.

The Catholicon which for some marks the Center of the World.

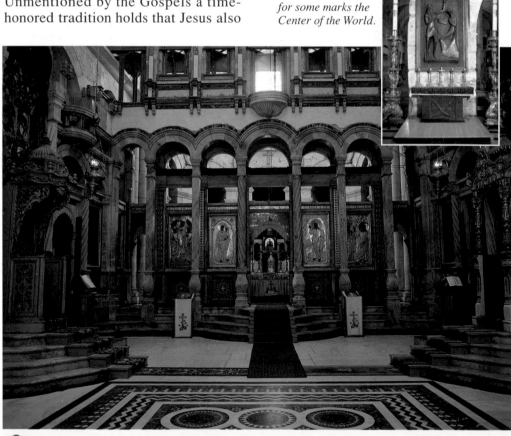

The Gospels and the book of Acts record eleven times that Jesus appeared following His resurrection. Tradition says that His first appearance before the disciples was on Mount Zion (pages 128/9) and for generations a Crusader chapel below the Cenacle recalled the Apparition of the Risen Christ. Described by John this was on Sunday night in Jerusalem, *"where the disciples were assembled ... came Jesus and stood in the midst, and saith unto them, Peace be unto you. And when he had so said, he shewed unto them his hands and his side. And the disciple were glad, when they saw the Lord"*, John 20:19-20. The disciple Thomas was not with them that evening, and he was only to see the risen Christ eight days

The Latin rites are practiced by many orders of the Roman Catholics.

A colorful Armenian procession.

later when his doubts were overcome by the evidence of his physical senses.

For generations the custodianship of the Church of the Holy Sepulchre has been divided between the five Christian communities: Roman Catholics, Greek Orthodox, Armenian, Copts and Syrian Orthodox. Ethiopian monks have cells and a chapel in the old Crusader refectory alongside the church.

Jesus showing his wounds to Doubting Thomas, depicted on a Crusader column from Nazareth.

The Greek Orthodox Ceremony of the Fire.

GORDON'S CALVARY

And The Garden Tomb

Looking out from the walls of Jerusalem's Old City the famous British general, Gordon of Khartoum, saw the resemblance to a human skull in a nearby rock formation. After he found there an ancient tomb surrounded by a garden below a small hill

This bricked up opening marks the entrance to the tomb.

Detail of the interior of the tomb.

Charles Gordon became convinced that this was the true Calvary, site of the Crucifixion. Since that day in 1 8 8 3 m a n y Protestants - especially those of the worldwide Church of England community - have seen **Gordon's Calvary** as the true site of Jesus' crucifixion and burial, in preference to the spot marked in the Holy Sepulchre and revered by Catholics and the Orthodox Church.

The debate centers around the fact that not only is the original site of Golgotha not known - it only having being said by John's Gospel to be *"nigh to the city"* - but neither does anyone know where the wall of Jerusalem actually stood in those days. Despite the conclusion of modern archaeologists that the Garden Tomb does date back to the 1st century AD, most

The Garden surrounds a typical 1st century Jewish tomb.

Britain's General Gordon saw the skull of Golgotha in these rock formations.

Biblical scholars are reluctant to dismiss the traditional site of the Holy Sepulchre as being the place described by the Gospels.

In 1894 the site of what has become known as Gordon's Calvary was acquired by Garden Tomb Association, formed and headquartered in London "for the preservation of the Tomb and Garden outside the walls of Jerusalem, believed by many to be the Sepulchre and garden of Joseph of Arimathea … that it might be kept sacred as a quiet spot".

EMMAUS

The Resurrection

The location of **Emmaus** has for long been a mystery, and therefore several villages have carried the name. In the 3rd century AD it was placed at present-day **Latrun** - a small rise overlooking the fertile Plains of Ayalon below the foothills of Jerusalem. A village called Emmaus had existed there since the Greek period. In Byzantine times it grew to become a city renamed Nicopolis, and in the 12th century the Crusaders incorporated the remains of the earlier mosaic floor into their own Romanesque church.

Detail of a mosaic from the original Byzantine church.

At the end of the 19th century a beautiful Trappist monastery was erected on a nearby

And behold, two of them went that same day to a village called Emmaus, which was from Jerusalem about three-score furlongs. And they talked together of all these things which had happened. And it came to pass that, while they communed together and reasoned, Jesus himself drew near, and went with them. ... And it came to pass, as he sat at meat with them, he took bread, and blessed it, and brake, and gave to them. And their eyes were opened, and they knew him; and he vanished out of their sight.

Luke 24:13-15; 30-31

hillside. Famous for its wine, the area is full of the remains of a large Crusader castle that once housed Richard the Lionheart. Some of the underground chambers on the brow of the hill remain undisturbed. Originally called Le Toron de Chavaliers - the Knights' Tower - this title gave the name Latrun.

Remains of the impressive Crusader church at Latrun.

international music festival and frequent weekend choral concerts.

A third site recognized as Emmaus is the Arab village of **Qubeibeh**, twelve miles northwest of Jerusalem. Tradition calls the church here **the House of Cleopas**, one of the two men who met Jesus that day. Here also the Crusaders erected a church upon Byzantine ruins, built over the foundations of an ancient room. Extensive remains dated to the 2-3 centuries BC and later Roman times were unearthed here. The Franciscans especially believe these mark the true site of Emmaus where the three sat to share a meal - an event recalled in a painting inside the church.

This statue of the Madonna and Child looks out over Abu Gosh.

The Crusaders however favored a site in present-day **Abu Gosh**, a picturesque village in the hills closer to Jerusalem. **The Church of the Resurrection** that they built covers an ancient Roman cistern. Inside the austere building beautiful medieval frescos, damaged by time, are now being restored and preserved.

With an imposing statue of the Madonna and Child, **the Church of Our Lady of the Ark of the Covenant** stands at the entrance to Abu Gosh. It is the venue for a renowned

The graceful lines of Latrun's Trappist monastery.

> After these things Jesus shewed himself again to the disciples at the Sea of Tiberias; ... when the morning was now come, Jesus stood on the shore: but the disciples knew not that it was Jesus. Then Jesus saith unto them, Children, have ye any meat? They answered him, No. And he said unto them, Cast the net on the right side of the ship, and ye shall find. They cast therefore, and now they were not able to draw it for the multitude of fishes.
>
> John 21:1-6

A modern statue echoes Jesus' words to Peter "thou shalt stretch forth thy hands, and another shall gird thee", John 21:16.

Inside the chapel, the Mensa Christi - the Table of Christ - is clearly visible.

In 1934, continuing an age-old tradition, the Franciscans dedicated a modest black basalt chapel at **Tabgha** on the shores of Lake Tiberias. Since the 4th century AD a **Chapel of the Primacy of St. Peter** has stood here, marking the spot that holds the memory of Jesus' third appearance to the disciples. It was here that He directed the disciples where to cast their nets to catch one hundred and fifty three fish; here that they then shared a meal upon a natural stone called Mensa Christi - Christ's Table - that still stands in the middle of the church; and here that Jesus appointed Simon Peter to the leadership of the early church.

The simple Chapel of the Primacy of St. Peter celebrates the third appearance of the resurrected Christ.

On the Mount of Olives

The Gospel of Luke, the Book of Acts 1:12 and tradition all place the Ascension of Jesus to heaven on the Mount of Olives. The original Church of the Ascension was built about 380 AD by a pious Roman matriarch named Pomenia. She erected a large circular shrine at the site open to the sky, called **the Imbomon**. By the sixth century the mountain top was teeming with nuns and monks who attended both this church and the nearby Eleona - the great Basilica of the Mount of Olives raised by Constantine's mother Queen Helena over the Grotto of the Inscrutable Mysteries (pages 114/5). These churches, along with at least half a dozen monasteries, were destroyed in 614 when the Persian hoardes massacred over 1200 Christians on the Mount of Olives on their way into Jerusalem.

Upon these ruins the Crusaders designed an octagonal **Church of the Ascension**, built atop a platform reached up a flight of 20 steps. Its beautifully dressed arches - all that is left of their church - created an inner courtyard that was also open to the sky. Here beneath the altar still stands the sacred rock on which tradition sees the imprint left by Jesus' foot as He ascended into heaven.

After Saladin retook Jerusalem in 1187 the Moslems closed the roof and the building was turned into a mosque. Today the various Christian denominations mark the Feast of the Ascension here every year 40 days after Easter with prayers around the sacred rock.

During the 19th century, the Russian Orthodox Church was one of the most active in the Holy Land. Building many churches, and over 100 schools in the Galilee alone, they also erected their own shrine to the Ascension further along the summit of the Mount of Olives. In the

And he said unto them, Thus it is written, and thus it behoved Christ to suffer, and to rise from the dead the third day: And that repentance and remission of sins should be preached in his name among all nations, beginning at Jerusalem. ... And he led them out as far as to Bethany, and he lifted up his hands, and blessed them. And it came to pass, while he blessed them, he was parted from them, and carried up into heaven.

Luke 24:46-51

The dome of the Church of the Ascension was closed when it was turned into a mosque in 1187.

custody of Russian nuns since 1907, its six storey tower, reached up 214 steps, affords the most extensive view across Jerusalem. An ancient mosaic and a small museum complete a worthwhile visit - one that is especially recommended around 4.30 p.m. when the nuns sing Vespers in a beautiful Russian chant.

The Russian Orthodox Church of the Ascension stands on Byzantine ruins with many fine mosaics.

MEGIDDO

The site of Armageddon

Built, destroyed and rebuilt more than twenty times over 6,000 years, **Megiddo** is the battlefield of history. The place of mankind's earliest recorded battle, Megiddo is mentioned in Revelations by the name **Armageddon** (from Har Megiddo meaning Mount Megiddo). It is the site of the final confrontation between good and evil.

Overlooking the fertile Jezreel Valley and guarding the strategic and lucrative route between Egypt and Mesopotamia, it was inevitable that Megiddo would be constantly fought over. First inhabited during Neolithic times, Megiddo was fortified by the Canaanites around 2,000 BC. Two centuries later it was a stronghold of the Hittites, Shepherd Kings who invaded both Palestine and Egypt. In the 15th century BC Egyptian pharaoh Thutmose III led a great army across the Sinai Desert. Marching up the Mediterranean coast and inland he defeated the assembled "Princes of the North" beneath Megiddo's walls. With a detailed account of both the journey

A tunnel leads down to the large water cistern that allowed the city to withstand numerous sieges.

and the combat itself etched on the walls of the Temple of Karnak in Luxor, the victory at Megiddo is the earliest single battle (as opposed to campaign or war) ever to be recorded.

The famous Tel el Amarna tablets contain letters written by the Governor of Megiddo asking the help of pharaoh Amenophis III. He was being harassed by bands of *Hapiru*, believed to be the original Hebrews. Later King David defeated the Philistines bringing Megiddo into his flourishing Israelite kingdom, and his son Solomon, who extended Israel's commercial network, made Megiddo one of his administrative centers.

It was the Biblical mention of Solomon's 1,400 chariots (1 Kings 10:26) stationed in his cities that led early archaeologists to conclude they had found Solomon's Stables in Megiddo. It is now reasoned that so many horses were probably stabled outside the city walls, not within. Megiddo is one of Israael's most extensive ongoing digs and **the Museum of Megiddo** has a model and many displays showing the tel before and after Solomon's reign.

A deep cut shows where archaeologists have dug through twenty layers of occupation.

*Mount Megiddo stands protectively over
the fertile plains of the Jezreel Valley.*

Even in the First World War Megiddo
figured as a battleground. It was fought
over as the British general Allenby swept
the Turkish forces north from Jerusalem
back as far as Damascus, before they
broke completely as he pushed on towards
Constantinople. For his work he was
granted the title Allenby, Lord of Megiddo.

*For they are the spirits of devils,
working miracles, which go forth
unto the kings of the earth and of
the whole world, to gather them
to the battle of that great day of
God Almighty. ... And he gathered
them together into a place called
in the Hebrew tongue Armageddon.*

Revelation 16:14-16

Israel
Today

JERUSALEM

The Jewish Quarter

Following the total destruction of Jerusalem in 135 AD, Emperor Hadrian forbade Jews to even enter the new Roman city he raised in its place. But, dispersed throughout the empire, the Jews kept Jerusalem forever in their hearts. Returning to the Promised Land in the 19th century they re-settled the Old City's **Jewish Quarter** until the 1948 War of Independence left it once again destroyed, and under Jordanian control. June 1967 saw a wave of joy surge through the Jewish world as Jerusalem was reunified and **the Kotel**, the Hebrew name for **the Western Wall** (pages 106/7) and other revered sites returned into Jewish hands. An extensive program of reconstruction and archaeological exploration of the Jewish Quarter followed.

The Wohl Archaeological Museum displays remains of homes of the Herodian Quarter from Second Temple times. Restored mosaics, period furniture and other artifacts show how people lived two thousand years ago. The nearby **Burnt House** is the ruins of a seven-roomed dwelling that belonged to the Kathros priestly family. It was gutted in 70 ẠD when Titus' troops torched Jerusalem's Second Temple and the main residential district.

One can walk along **the Cardo**, the main street of the Byzantine city reconstructed in the 5th century on the lines of Hadrian's Aelia Capitolina. Discovered with the help of a mosaic map found at Madaba (pages 186/7) the Cardo once ran from the Damascus Gate to where the ruins of the Nea Church are seen today by the Zion Gate. Modern shops bring this ancient arcade back to life.

Upon the ruins of three high towers that once guarded King Herod's palace close to the Temple, the 12th century Crusaders built **the Citadel** in their typical fortress style. But even the surrounding moat did not prevent it being destroyed by the Moslems in the 13th century. Finally the Ottoman Turks rebuilt the Citadel next to the Jaffa

The Hurva - ruins of a synagogue said to be the "window to heaven".

David's Tower above the Citadel is actually a 17th century Moslem minaret.

Gate, and added the minaret known as **the Tower of David**. One of the city's most famous landmarks, it now houses a unique museum dedicated to the history of Jerusalem. Here modern exhibits are complemented by ancient surroundings, and on summer nights a sound and light show is held in the fine Mameluk and Ottoman courtyard.

Part of the colonnade of the Cardo - the main street of Byzantine Jerusalem.

Its ceiling resting on four Byzantine pillars, for generations the 13th century **Ramban Synagogue** was the Jews' only house of prayer in the city. Naturally it became the hub of the Jewish Quarter. That title is now claimed by the Hurva Square built by the remains of **the Hurva**, an 18th century synagogue about which it was said *"As the Temple Mount is the gateway to Heaven, so the Hurva is its window"*. Burned down, rebuilt and then destroyed again in 1948, the Hurva has been left as a ruin with just a single arch restored. Nearby is a complex of four restored **Sephardic Synagogues** originally built by Jews expelled by the Spanish Inquisition of the 16th century.

Remains of the Burnt House destroyed by the Romans at the time of First Revolt.

Jerusalem is the third holiest city of Islam. Its status rests on the fact that the prophet Mohammed originally told his followers to pray facing the city where, according to the Koran, he was taken on his "Night Journey", *"Glory be to him who made His servant go by night from the Sacred Temple (Mecca) to the farther Temple (Jerusalem) whose surroundings we have blessed"*, Sutra 17:1. Situated on the Temple Mount, those surroundings are known in Arabic as Haram al-Sharif, the Noble Sanctuary - the heart of Moslem Jerusalem.

Caliph Omar ibn-al-Khattab, the second leader of Islam after Mohammed, conquered the Holy Land from the crumbling Byzantine world. Entering Jerusalem in 638 AD he cleared the ruins of the ancient Temple and built there a simple Moslem mosque.

This was described two years later by the Christian pilgrim, Arculf, who wrote, *"In that renowned place where once the Temple had been magnificently constructed, … the Saracens now prepared a quadrangular place of prayer which they have built rudely constructed by setting great beams on some remains of ruins"*.

It was the Ummayad caliph al-Walid who originally erected the great **Al Aqsa Mosque** above this shrine between 705 and 715. Damaged by repeated earthquakes it was rebuilt by the caliph of Egypt, al-Zahir, in 1035 who gave the structure much of its present form. When the Crusaders took the city soon after they renamed the mosque the Temple of Solomon, and turned it into the headquarters of the first and fiercest group of fighting monks - the Order of the Knights Templar. They added their own touch to the mosque and many fine structures to the precinct, but most of these were unfortunately destroyed during the last century.

Designed around the sacred number seven, the Al Aqsa mosque is a classic example of Islam's geometric architecture.

Saladin, who recaptured the city, the Mameluks, Ayyubis and the later Ottoman rulers, all took a hand in giving the mosque a mixed style unique in Islamic architecture. The final touches to the Al Aqsa came in 1939 when the ceiling was redecorated as a gift from Egypt's last monarch, King Faroukh.

Originally built in 705 AD, the Al Aqsa is the largest mosque in Jerusalem.

Known as Solomon's Stables the mosque's underground vaults were used by the Crusader Order of the Knights Templar, founded in 1118.

THE DOME OF THE ROCK

When the victorious Caliph Omar ibn-al-Khattab entered the Temple Mount in 638 he knelt and immediately began clearing away the accumulated rubble of centuries - using the hem of his own robe. Joined by his followers, they soon revealed **the Rock** - *al-Sakhra* - from which the prophet Mohammed stepped up to the Seventh Heaven to stand before God on his "Night Journey". This is the same Rock upon which Abraham is said to have prepared to sacrifice his son. Though the Bible recounts that this was Isaac (Genesis 22), Moslem tradition relates that it was his first-born son Ishmael who was about to be sacrificed.

A special cabinet houses what many believe is a hair from Mohammed's beard.

In 688 the fifth Ummayad caliph, Abd al-Malik, began work on the sublimely created **Dome of the Rock**. Ruling most of the Islamic world from Damascus, but without Mecca and Medina, he desperately wanted to undermine the power of his enemies. In a bid to make Jerusalem the new center of Moslem pilgrimage, Abd al-Malik invested seven years' income from the rich province of Egypt.

Standing out below the new golden dome, a gift from Jordan's late King Hussein, are evocative verses from the Koran.

Abd-al-Malik's original tiles were replaced long ago. Local Armenian craftsmen made the latest ones in 1963.

Employing Byzantine and local Christian experts and labor brought in from Egypt he raised a golden-domed monument 180 feet high (55m) over the Rock to outshine anything in the Islamic world - or in Christendom.

Based on the design principles of the Holy Sepulchre, constructed of stone and marble, sumptuously decorated with mosaics and glazed tiles bearing entire chapters of the Koran and illuminated by 36 stained-glass windows, the Dome of the Rock became the centerpiece for all Islamic ceremonies in Jerusalem. In the same way as they circled the Black Stone of the Ka'ba in Mecca, Moslem pilgrims filled with wonder as they walked seven times around the Rock from where tradition says a trumpet will sound on Judgement Day, and where the Gates of Heaven will open.

The Holy month of Ramadan calls the Faithful to the Noble Sanctuary for daily prayers.

Once the base of the altar in Solomon's Temple, the Faithful see in the Rock Mohammed's footprint and the mark of the hand of the Angel Gabriel. Beneath it a large cavern called **the Well of the Souls** is where the spirits of the dead gather to join Friday prayers.

Built over the site of the ancient Hebrew Temple, the heart of the Rock is where Abraham is said to have brought his son for sacrifice, and from where Mohammed is believed to have ascended to heaven.

In the time of the Kingdom of Jerusalem, the Crusaders renamed the Dome of the Rock *Templum Domini* - the Temple of the Lord - and transformed it into a church, raising a great golden cross on its dome in place of the Moslem crescent moon. Restored to Islam by Saladin, the next major change came with the arrival of the Ottoman sultan Suleiman the Magnificent (1520-66). In 1552 he replaced the old external mosaics with new azure-blue tiles fired in the renowned Persian kilns of Kashan. The inscribed texts from the Koran inside were executed in 1876 by the famed Turkish calligrapher, Mohammed Chafik.

Moslem traditions abound both about the Rock and about Jerusalem as a whole. They say that the Rock was the first thing to appear out of the waters of the Flood; that whoever offers even the shortest prayer in Jerusalem secures a place in Paradise; and that on Judgement Day the shrine of Mecca - the holy black Ka'ba - will be brought in a triumphal procession like a bride to Jerusalem. Laid out in three concentric sections marking the passage from the mundane to the divine, the Dome of the Rock, like a waiting bridegroom, stands ready to welcome its arrival.

HARAM AL-SHARIF

The Noble Sanctuary

Entered by one of fifteen gates **the Haram al-Sharif - the Noble Sanctuary** is a feast of aesthetic architecture based on Islamic sacred geometric design. Dominated by the harmonic proportions of the octagonal Dome of the Rock - created by two squares offset by 45^0 - all the lesser structures were erected to reflect and enhance its glory.

In the mid 13th century a new force arose in the Arab world. Whole generations of slave children brought from the Caucasus region and reared as soldiers had risen to become the generals of Egypt's army. These Mameluks had bought their freedom and now ousted the Ayyubid successors of Saladin (1171-1250). Taking control of the powerful state they began a plan of territorial expansion. They brought down the remains of the Crusader Kingdom backed by the English and French kings Richard the Lionheart and Louis IX. In 1291 they took the capital St. Jean d'Acre finally putting an end to the Frankish presence in the Holy Land.

Fed by a huge cistern under the plaza, the al-Kads fountain allows Moslems to ritually wash head, hands and feet before praying.

The 30 acre Haram al-Sharif - the precinct of the ancient Hebrew Temple - is dominated by the octagonal Dome of the Rock, often mistakenly called the Mosque of Omar.

Black and white decorations, some with red accents, are classic examples of Mameluk design.

During that time the Mameluks also stopped the hordes of invading Asian Mongols who had conquered Syria and seemed set to sweep through both Palestine and Europe. From the victory at the Battle of Ein Harod (1260) in the Jezreel Valley (page 73), the Mameluks drove the Mongols back beyond the Euphrates. Maintaining power till Selim I arrived in 1517 and began four hundred years of Ottoman rule, much of the Noble Sanctuary was constructed by Mameluk hands.

Receding archways echo the Sanctuary's sense of the infinite.

Perhaps the finest example of Mameluk architecture is this fountain built by the 15th century sultan Qayt Bey.

On the southern side of the plaza is a building once called the **Mosque of the Moors.** Originally built in 1194 by Saladin's son al-Afdal, today it houses the interesting **Islamic Museum**. Also worth a visit is the exquisite **Museum of Islamic** Art on Hapalmach St. in the West Jerusalem suburb of Rechavia.

MODERN JERUSALEM

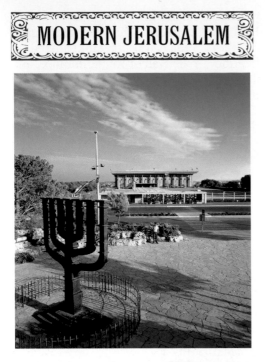

Age-old symbol of the Jewish people, this Menorah stands as a sentinel next to the Knesset, Israel's parliament.

The Menorah

Together with the Star of David, the Menorah is one of the two symbols used by the Jewish people for thousands of years (Beth Shearim photo, page 80). This large bronze Menorah, work of the sculptor Benno Elkan, was a gift from the British Parliament donated in 1956. Standing next to the Israel's young parliament building, the sculpture depicts twenty-nine vivid scenes from Jewish history, ancient and modern: Moses, whose outstretched arms ensured the presence of God with the people during battle; the young King David holding the head of the Philistine giant, Goliath; and the Holocaust of the Second World War which preceded the establishment of the modern state of Israel. It is inscribed with the words, *"The Menorah is a symbol of the light of faith and hope which has led the Jewish people for four thousand years"*.

Mishkanot Sha'ananim

In the mid 19th century, European Jews began returning to their Promised Land and it was not long before the Old City became too small for Jerusalem's rapidly expanding population. Built with the help of philanthropist Sir Moses Montefiore, they called the first Jewish suburb outside the walls, Mishkanot Sha'ananim, the Dwellings of the Tranquil. The windmill was designed to provide work but being built too low on the hillside its sails never turned in the wind. Despite this inauspicious start, Mishkanot Sha'ananim, also called Yemin Moshe, eventually blossomed and the windmill became one of Jerusalem's most famous modern landmarks.

With its familiar windmill Yemin Moshe was the first Jewish suburb built outside the Old City walls.

Jerusalem's relatively cool climate is a blessing for the thriving cosmopolitan city.

Yad Vashem

An eternal flame burns night and day in the heart of Jerusalem. This is Yad Vashem, Israel's memorial to the 6 million Jews who perished during the horrors of the Nazi Holocaust of World War Two. The names of all the death camps are emblazoned on the floor of the Hall of Remembrance, and the name of every known victim is enshrined in Yad Vashem's museum. This museum documents the rise of Hitler's National Socialist Party and the atrocities it committed during its years in power. It also records the heroic acts of those who fought against them - like those who took part in the Warsaw Ghetto uprising.

Survivors, victims' families and the whole nation gather here, to remember lost loved ones or to honor the many non-Jews who risked their own lives helping Jews escape. One of these is Dr. Janusz Korczak, the Polish educator who valiantly tried saving the lives of orphan children. It is his face that is immortalized at the entrance to the Children's memorial. In this way Yad Vashem keeps alive the memory of the Holocaust for the whole world.

This sculpture stands at the entrance to the Children's memorial.

In the Hall of Remembrance an eternal flame burns in memory of the victims of Nazi persecution.

TEL AVIV/JAFFA

Jaffa's 4,000 year old port is one of the oldest in the world.

Tel Aviv

Founded in 1909 by sixty Jewish families on the empty sand dunes just north of the ancient town of Jaffa, Tel Aviv means the Hill of Spring. Blending an architectural style that marries the Middle East environment with the European roots of many of its original settlers, Tel Aviv expanded to become Israel's commercial and cultural center. It was here that the newly independent state of Israel was declared in May 1948.

Excavations north of the city uncovered the ancient settlement of **Tel Qasila**, and led to the creation of **the Eretz Israel Museum** in Ramat Aviv. Tracing the history of Mediterranean life from prehistoric times, the museum displays finds in several attractive pavilions, each dedicated to a different theme - pottery and ceramics, glass, coins, ethnology and folklore. The nearby **Museum of the Diaspora** (Bet Hatfutsot) is dedicated to the 2,000 year history of the Jewish people since the destruction of the Second Temple.

Some of Tel Aviv's beachside cafes.

Tel Aviv is a sparkling city seen from the air - or from the ground.

Today, Tel Aviv is the country's largest and most cosmopolitan metropolis - a paradise for those that love combining the delights of the city and the pleasures of the Mediterranean's sunny beaches.

Jaffa

Although integrated with modern Tel Aviv, the ancient port of Jaffa carries an atmosphere very much its own. Dating back around four millennia it is steeped in history. It was from here that Jonah set off on his voyage that ended in the belly of a whale. It was through Jaffa that King Solomon imported the Cedars of Lebanon. And it was to Jaffa that St. Peter came to stay in the house of Simon the Tanner and raise Tabitha from the dead (Acts 9:39-43). An earlier Greek legend tells that the beautiful goddess Andromeda was bound to a rock in Jaffa harbor as a sacrifice to a horrible sea monster, till she was saved by the hero Perseus.

This fountain is in a piazza named after Tel Aviv's first mayor, Meir Dizengoff.

At the end of the 19th century Jaffa became a gateway to the new wave of European tourism pioneered by the likes of Cooke's Tours and Baron Ustinoff, the grandfather of the famous actor Peter Ustinoff, who owned one of the first hotels in the town. **Old Jaffa** boasts an attractively reconstructed Artists Quarter, flea market, and a wide range of appetizing restaurants especially on the harbor front.

HAIFA

Built along the slopes of Mount Carmel overlooking the Mediterranean Sea, **Haifa** is another port town dating from antiquity. In modern times it has grown to become Israel's third largest city and the heart of the country's heavy industry. In recent years Haifa has shone as an international hub of hi-tech development in computer- and bio-technologies. Led by the Technion (Israel's Institute of Technology) the Haifa University and the Carmel Medical Center, together with the commercial Center for Advance Technologies (Matam) - Haifa has attracted the R & D facilities of some of the world's premier companies such as Microsoft, IBM and Intel.

Israel's coastline seen from Rosh Hanikra, 26 miles (42 kms) north of Haifa.

Haifa is also the world center of the Bahai faith. Founded in Persia in the 19th century this religion unites all monotheistic teachings. The famous golden domed temple is the exquisite shrine of its founder, the Bab, meaning Gate or Forerunner. This is the name given to Mizra Ali Muhammed who was executed for his teachings in 1850 at the age of 30. Both the shrine and the nearby world administrative center, called the Universal House of Justice, are surrounded by beautifully laid out gardens that are a pleasure to visit.

Outside Haifa, southwards on the crest of the Carmel range, are the picturesque villages of Dalyat el-Carmel and Isfaya. These are communities of the Druze religion that dates back to the 10th century Egyptian caliph, al-Hakkim. Thought of as a splinter of Islam, the Druze maintain their own identity around a teaching so secret that it is known only to the initiates among their own people.

The caves of Rosh Hanikra on the Lebanese border.

These men are "Ok'al", initiates into the secretive Druze religion.

The Bahai Temple overlooks the slopes of Haifa's Carmel Mountain and the bay below.

EILAT

The southernmost city in Israel, Eilat is blessed with the glorious waters of the Gulf of Aqaba - the eastern tip of the Red Sea. In Biblical times King Solomon's fleet sailed out of *"Ezion-geber which is by Eloth, on the shore of the Red Sea"* to bring back 420 talents of gold from Ofir, thought to be either Ethiopia or India (1Kings 9). Today Eilat is again a serious port, providing the country with a trade route to Asia, but it has bloomed most as the Israeli riveria. Sunny and warm in winter and hot but dry during the summer, Eilat is a year-round paradise for holiday-makers -and the entry-point to Egypt's Sinai desert (pages 30-33).

Hotels, sandy beaches, yachts, coral reefs and endless desert beyond.

The reef is an ever-changing kaleidoscope of color and shape.

The Coral World Underwater Observatory invites visitors into another world.

Bare desert mountains line the coast in stark contrast to the deep-blue waters and the multi-colored coral reef just yards from the shore. This can be experienced snorkel or scuba diving, explored from a glass-bottomed boat, or marveled at in the Underwater Observatory.

Eilat offers every water-sport and beachside amenity conceivable - all that a traveler could wish for.

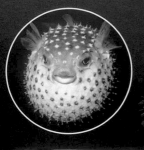

One of the many species of tropical fish swimming on the reef.

Two-thirds of the Holy Land is waterless desert. Now called **the Judean** and **Negev deserts**, in the Bible they are named the Wilderness of Paran and of Zin. Although unmentioned by the Gospels these regions were far more populous in those days than they are now. A land-link between continents these deserts are the limit of the habitats of many European, African and Asian creatures - and the migratory route for many birds. In recent years a special nature reserve was set up just north of Eilat to protect endangered species.

Inhospitable at first sight, the desert's natural beauty shines all year-round. In winter, natural pools form in otherwise dry river valleys called Wadis, and wildflowers spring up after the rains, blossoming like a multi-colored carpet. In summer the sun turns rock and sand formations into different pastel shades in the evening - or hides them with shimmering heat waves in the middle of the day. Even

The "mushroom" at the Timna Park is near mines that produced copper for over 6,000 years.

nights are a wonder as the moon floats in a canopy of stars that seem to sit just out of reach.

Orynx and other endangered species thrive in the Hai Bar nature reserve.

Sudden winter showers swiftly
fill otherwise dry river beds.

An Egyptian temple dedicated to the
goddess Hathor was uncovered by
these "Pillars of Solomon".

JERASH

In the Hashemite Kingdom of Jordan

Jerash - ancient Gerasa - lies about 24 miles (40 km) north of present day Amman. Excavations carried out since the early 1920's have uncovered much about the history of the city. Built on the Biblical Kings Highway - the ancient trade route that ran from the Gulf of Aqaba up to Damascus - Jerash has been populated from around the third millennium BC.

This elegant mosque is a source of pride for Jerash's modern community ...

... just as the Roman Forum was for ancient Jerash.

More than 250 columns once lined the main throughway.

Jerash reached its zenith under the Seleucid successors to Alexander the Great who built a completely new city here after defeating their rivals, the Ptolomies. Following a short period under the Jewish rule of the Hasmonean king, Alexander Janneus, the expanding Roman Empire made Jerash part of the Decapolis, a league of ten cities mentioned in the Gospels (pages 72/3). Jewish Zealots took Jerash during the First Revolt but failed to hold it in the face of the crushing power of Vespasian's legionnaires. Flourishing during the Byzantine period, Jerash has seen mixed fortunes in the fourteen centuries since it came under Moslem rule in 630 AD.

Stone work shows excellent craftsmanship.

Falconry is a royal sport still practised by the Hashemites.

MADABA

In the Hashemite Kingdom of Jordan

A column base bears witness to the Roman presence here.

The ancient Jordanian town of **Madaba** has a proud and prosperous history. Sitting on the same important trade route as Jerash, it too flourished early in the first Millennium. In the 6th century AD Madaba boasted a large church with an exquisite mosaic floor. Discovered by accident in the 19th century the floor depicts a remarkable map of the Holy Land. Despite the ravages of time it still shows many of the important sites - the Jordan River, Dead Sea, Jericho, Bethlehem and many more places are all clearly visible. The map of Jerusalem is so accurately illustrated - with fine details of the Cardo and the Holy Sepulchre - that it recently helped archaeologists pinpoint the long lost site of the Church of Theotokos, the Nea or New Church destroyed by the Persians in 614.

Detail of Jerusalem: the Cardo runs across with the Holy Sepulchre inverted below it.

Madaba's mosaic map shows the Dead Sea at the top and Jerusalem in the center.

MOUNT NEBO

In the Hashemite Kingdom of Jordan

Of no awesome height, Mount Nebo takes its majesty from the widely-held belief that it was here that Moses was granted his only view of the Promised Land. According to the Bible it was on this mountain on the eastern side of the Dead Sea that Moses died, forbidden by God to enter the Promised Land that he had led the Children of Israel out of Egypt to achieve. Nearby an attractive spring bears his name. Moses was buried in a place that the Bible says no one shall ever know … but he left behind him a religious and moral code that has continued to guide the western world for more than three thousand years.

Originally marked by a small chapel, by the 6th century a prestigious monastery had grown up here.

From this spot Moses looked over the Promised Land he was not to enter.

And Moses went up from the plains of Moab unto the mountain of Nebo … and the Lord showed him … all the land of Gilead unto Dan … and all the land of Judah, unto the uttermost sea … And the Lord said unto him, This is the land which I sware unto Abraham, unto Isaac and unto Jacob, saying, I will give it unto thy seed: …. I have caused thee to see it with thine eyes, but thou shalt not go over thither. Deuteronomy 34:1-5

"And the Children of Israel wept for Moses in the plains of Moab thirty days…. And there arose not a prophet since in Israel like unto Moses, whom the Lord knew face to face", Deuteronomy 34:8 & 10. Not, that is, until the coming of the Lord Jesus Christ.

This beautiful mosaic floor was discovered by Franciscan archaeologists.

TIME LINE

Prehistory: The Stone Age ends with the Neolithic Revolution. From Mesopotamia's Fertile Crescent to Egypt's Nile Valley agriculture and domestication of animals heralds widespread permanent settlement. Jericho established.
8000 - 5000 BC

Ancient Biblical History: City-states emerge, trade routes develop and Empires arise. Abraham migrates from Ur of the Chaldees in Mesopotamia to Canaan. Famine forces descendents to Egypt. Bronze Age Egypt expands northward bringing fortified Canaanite towns under its control.
5000 - 1200 BC

Israelite Period: Moses leads Exodus from Egypt. Joshua commands Israelite conquest of Promised Land. Judges rule the Twelve Tribes till they demand monarchy. David reigns growing Iron Age kingdom, defeats Philistine "Sea People", conquers Jerusalem and makes it capital. His son Solomon builds First Temple.
1200 - 900 BC

Assyria, Greece and Rome: Solomon dies, kingdom divided. Temple and Jerusalem destroyed by Assyrian invasion, people led captive to Babylon. Cyrus ends Exile, people return rebuilding Temple. Alexander the Great defeats Persia, spreads Greek culture but respects local religions. Repressive Seleucid successors ignite Maccabean revolt that re-establishes independent Jewish state ruled by Hasmonean dynasty. Pompey makes Judea buffer state for Rome.
900 - 63 BC

Herod, Jesus and the destruction of Jerusalem: Herod the Great rebuilds Second Temple but sons fail to hold kingdom. Divided Judea becomes Roman Province. Messianic expectations mark religious and political upheaval. Jew-despising Pontius Pilate made Prefect of Judea. Pilate crucifies Jesus, massacres Samaritans. Pilate sent home in dishonor, but unrest persists. Violent demonstrations become country-wide revolt. Jews take Masada and Jerusalem. 50,000 Roman soldiers put down insurrection, destroy Temple. After 60 years Second Revolt erupts. It is suppressed and Jerusalem is totally destroyed.
63 BC - 200 AD

Early Christianity & Byzantine: Emperor Constantine ends centuries of Roman persecution of Christians. His mother, Queen Helena, identifies Holy sites and builds first churches. Western Roman Empire falls, Eastern Empire ruled from Byzantium. Persians conquer Holy Land, destroy most churches. Byzantine regains Holy Land for a decade.
200 - 630 AD

Arab Conquests: Mohammed pronounces start of Islam. Within a generation Islam bursts from Arabia to occupy the Holy Land. Centuries of Arab rule make Jerusalem Islam's third holiest city. Seljuk Turks occupy Syria and Jerusalem, destroy churches and persecute Christian pilgrims.
630 - 1099 AD

The Crusades: Pope Urban II fires thousands to free Holy Land from the "infidels", starting centuries of Crusades. Kingdom of Jerusalem lasts less than 100 years but cements generations of Arab-Christian hatred. Saladin leads *jihad* to recapture Jerusalem. Richard the Lionheart leads 3rd Crusade: fails to retake city but secures continued Latin presence. Saladin's Ayyubid successors tolerate Crusaders, but Mameluks who follow them do not.
1099 - 1250 AD

Mameluks: Former Turkish slave-warriors rise to power in Egypt, defeat the invading Mongols then drive last Crusaders out of Acre. Fine architectural legacy, but Jerusalem sees economic decline while remaining center of Arab scholarship. Mameluks rule till defeated by new power from the north.
1250 - 1517 AD

Ottoman Empire: Stretching from Macedonia to Arabia Ottoman Turks rule for 400 years. Suleimann the Magnificent (1520-66) rebuilds walls of Jerusalem and repairs many other shrines but later governors allow city and province to decline. In 1799 Napoleon Bonaparte tries to invade Syria, but is defeated at Acre. 19th century European powers vie for control as Eastern European Jews begin a return to Zion.
1517 - 1900 AD

The State of Israel: World War I. General Allenby occupies Holy Land, League of Nations grants Britain a Mandate to rule Palestine. Decades of unrest and the Nazi Holocaust of World War II cause UN to vote for a Jewish state. May 14 1948 David Ben Gurion proclaims the creation of the State of Israel. Decades of war followed by peace with Egypt, then Jordan. New millennium opens amid uneasy negotiations with Palestinians and a withdrawal from Lebanon.
1917 - 2000 AD

Bibliography and Recommended Reading

Ancient Israel: A Short History from Abraham to the Roman Destruction of the Temple, ed. H. Shanks (Prentice Hall 1988)
Arab Historians of the Crusades, F. Gabrieli (Routledge & Kegan Paul 1984)
Archaeological Discoveries in the Holy Land, J. Pritchard, E. Anati, F. Cross Jr, K. Kenyon, Y. Yadin et al (Bonanza, Archaeological Institute of America 1962)
Archaeological Discoveries, Relative to the Judaeo-Christians, Fr. E. Testa (Franciscan Printing Press, Jerusalem)
The Archaeology of Palestine, W.F. Albright (Pelican 1960)
The Architecture of Ancient Israel: from the Prehistoric to the Persian Periods, Israel Exploration Society (Jerusalem 1992)
The Architecture of Petra, J. Mackenzie (Oxford U. Press 1990)
The Atlas of the Crusades, ed. J. Riley-Smith (Times Books 1991)
Bar-Kochba, Yigal Yadin, (London 1978)
Bible Lands, J. Tubb (Dorling Kindersley & the British Museum 1994)
The Birth of Israel, A. Laurie, from A History of the Holy Land (Jerusalem 1969)
The Canaanite and Israelite Periods, H. Reviv, from A History of the Holy Land (Jerusalem 1969)
Chronicles of the Crusades, Joinville & Villehardouin, tr. M. R. B. Shaw (Penguin 1963)
The Church of Circumcision, Fr. B. Bagatti (Franciscan Printing Press, Jerusalem)
The Church of the Gentiles, Fr. B. Bagatti (Franciscan Printing Press, Jerusalem)
Churches of the Holy Land, G. Bushell (Funk & Wagnalls 1969)
The Cross and the Crescent, M. Billings (BBC Books 1987)
The Crusades: A Short History, J. Riley-Smith (Athlone Press 1987)
The Crusades Through Arab Eyes, A. Maalouf (Al Saqi Books 1984)
The Day Christ Died, J. Bishop (Harper 1957)
The Dead Sea Scrolls in English, G. Vermes (Pelican 1986)
Digging up Jericho, K. Kenyon (Ernest Benn 1957)
The Earliest Lives of Jesus, R. Grant (Harper 1961)
Folklore of the Holy Land, Moslem, Christian and Jewish, J. Hanauer (London 1935)
The Gospels and the Jesus of History, X. Leon-Dufour (New York 1968)
Guide to the Holy Land, E. Hoade (Franciscan Printing Press, Jerusalem)
The Historical Geography of the Holy Land, G. Smith (Hodder & Stoughton 1894)
Historical Sites in Israel, M. Pearlman, Y. Yannai et al (Massada-PEC Press 1964)
The History of the Crusades, Sir S. Runciman (Cambridge U. Press 1951)
A History of the Holy Land, ed. M. Avi-Yonah (Jerusalem 1969)
The History of Islam, R. Payne (Dorset Press 1987)
The History of Palestine from the Arab Conquest until the Crusades, M. Sharon, from A History of the Holy Land (Jerusalem 1969)
The Holy Land, D. Roberts (Day & Son 1855)
Holy Places, C. Hollis and R. Brownrigg (Weidenfeld & Nicolson 1969)
The Holy Places of the Gospels, C. Kopp (New York 1962)
The Illustrated Atlas of Jerusalem, D. Bahat (Macmillan 1990)
In the Steps of the Master, H. Morton (London 1937)
Israel, F. Brenner (Collins Harvill 1988)
Israel: Years of Challenge, D. Ben Gurion (Blond 1979)
Jerusalem Architecture, Periods and Styles: 1860-1914, D. Kroyanker and D. Wahrman (Jerusalem 1983)
Jerusalem as Jesus Knew It: Archaeology as Evidence, J. Wilkinson (Thames & Hudson 1978)

Jerusalem: Excavating 3,000 years of History, K. Kenyon (Thames & Hudson 1967)
Jesus and His History, E. Stauffler (New York 1959)
Jesus in His Time, Daniel-Rops (Burns & Oates 1956)
Jesus of Nazareth, G. Bornkamm (New York 1960)
The Jewish War, Flavius Josephus, trans. G. A. Williamson (Harmondsworth 1978)
The Jewish World: Revelation, Prophecy and History, ed. E. Kedourie (Thames Hudson 1969)
The Jews: Their History, Culture and Religion, ed. L. Finkelstein (Philadelphia 1960)
John the Baptist, C. Kraeling (New York - London 1951)
The Jordan River, N. Glueck (Philadelphia 1946)
Judaism in Stone: the Archaeology of Ancient Synagogues, H. Shanks (Harper & Row 1979)
The Land of the Bible, a historical geography, Y. Aharoni, tr. A. Rainey (Burns & Oates 1967)
The Life of the Blessed Constantine, Eusebius of Caesarea (S. Bagster & Sons 1845)
The Life and Ministry of Jesus, V. Taylor (New York 1955)
Living in the Time of Jesus of Nazareth, P. Connolly, (Oxford U. Press 1983)
The Lion Handbook to the Bible, D. & P. Alexander (Lion 1983)
The Lord, R. Guardini (Longmans 1960)
The Making of the Middle Ages, R. Southern (Pimlico 1993)
Masada, Yigal Yadin, (London 1975)
Nazareth, M. Stiassny (Jerusalem Publishing House 1969)
Outremer: Studies in the History of the Crusading Kingdom of Jerusalem, ed. B. Kedar, H. Mayer, R. Smail (Yad Itzhak Ben-Zvi Institute, Jerusalem 1982)
The Oxford Dictionary of the Christian Church, ed. F.L. Cross & E.A. Livingstone (Oxford, 1983)
Palestine During the Crusades, E. Sivan, from A History of the Holy Land (Jerusalem 1969)
Palestine under the Mameluks and the Ottoman Empire, M. Sharon, from A History of the Holy Land (Jerusalem 1969)
The Passion and Death of Our Lord Jesus Christ, A. Goodier (Kennedy 1962)
Passion and Resurrection of Jesus Christ, P. Benoit (London 1969)
Petra, its History and its Monuments, A. Kennedy (London 1925)
The Prehistory of the Holy Land, E. Anati, from A History of the Holy Land (Jerusalem 1969)
The Pursuit of the Millennium: Revolutionary Millenarians and Mystical Anarchists of the Middle Ages, N. Cohn (Pimlico 1993)
The Second Temple, Jews, Romans and Byzantines, M. Avi-Yonah from A History of the Holy Land (Jerusalem 1969)
Seven Pillars of Wisdom, T. E. Lawrence (Cape 1976)
The Trial of Jesus, J. Blinzler (Cork 1959)
Western Pilgrims, E. Hoade (Franciscan Printing Press, Jerusalem)
With Jesus through Galilee according to the Fifth Gospel, B. Pixner (Corazim 1992)

Periodicals
Artifax, (Institute of Biblical Archaeology & Near East Archaeological Society)
The Biblical Archaeological Review, ed. H. Shanks (Biblical Archaeology Society)
Eretz – The Geographic Magazine, ed. M. Feinberg Vamosh (Israel)
Near Eastern Archaeology, ed. D. Hopkins (formerly Biblical Archaeologist, American Schools of Oriental Research)
Tel Aviv, ed. David Ussishkin (Institute of Archaeology, Tel Aviv U.)